ESSEX RIVERS AND CREEKS

Vol 4 English Estuaries Series

ROBERT SIMPER

Published in 1995 by Creekside Publishing
ISBN 0 8519927 4 0
copyright Robert Simper
Printed by The Lavenham Press Ltd
Lavenham, Suffolk

By the same author

Over Snape Bridge (1967)
Woodbridge & Beyond (1972)
East Coast Sail (1972)
Scottish Sail (1974)
North East Sail (1975)
Victorian & Edwardian Yachting from Old Photographs (1978)
Gaff Sail (1979)
Traditions of East Anglia (1980)
Suffolk Show (1981)
Britain's Maritime Heritage (1982)
Sail on the Orwell (1982)
Beach Boats of Britain(1984)
Sail. The Surviving Tradition (1984)
East Anglian Coast and Waterways (1985)
The Suffolk Sandlings (1986)
The Deben River (1992)
The River Orwell and the River Stour (1993)
Rivers Alde, Ore and Blyth (1994)
Woodbridge (1995)

CONTENTS

Cover: Aboard *L'Atalanta* anchored off Stone Point, 1988

Photograph by Jonathan Simper

ACKNOWLEDGEMENTS

She was trawling on the port tack and looked like something out of a nineteenth century oil painting. The smack's topsides were black and rough with countless coats of tar and the sails were old, faded and heavily patched. It was 1952 and I was making my first sea passage. Our skipper Arthur Hunt, who had been master of the barge *Dover Castle* until he had had a row with the owner Clem Parker on Bradwell Quay, saw nothing unusual about a smack trawling in the mouth of the Blackwater. We headed over towards the elderly smackmen, who looked even more ancient than their craft. While sorting out their gear, they gave us a modest wave and asked the time. They might just as well have asked which century it was, for although I did not realise it at the time, that lone smack was the last of her type working under sail.

This smack and the sailing barges coming down the Colne on the tide were the last remnants of the great age of coastal sail. They were part of the magic which belonged to the Essex estuaries. Remote areas were created by the four large estuaries and numerous creeks that cut into the Essex coastline. That remoteness still lingers on the Roach islands, Osea and other inaccessible places, but once the car and and the motorised yachts became available Essex was open to all to explore and settle.

Unfortunantly past generations had a very low regard for Essex. London sent its rubbish to be dumped on marshland, property developers made a quick buck knocking up cheap housing, river walls were torn down to flood areas which should have been saved. Essex was thought of as being the place where you could do anything you liked because it did not matter if you wrecked it. In fact people came here because they had the freedom to put up chalets near a creek, dig great holes for ballast or shoot all the wildfowl, as no one was going to take any notice. It has taken us to the end of the twentieth century to realise that the Essex coastal area and rivers have a very fragile environment which needs careful, and at times expensive, protection.

Certainly the coastal area of Essex is already sliding into becoming part of Greater London, pressure to retain its local identity must be kept up. The good news is that the Essex tidal rivers, although badly scarred in places, are large enough to have retained most their own very strong character. This book is an attempt to record the vital traditions of these rivers.

This very strong coastal culture was recognised by two authors who greatly influenced me. I knew James Wentworth Day and Hervey Benham and both helped me, but they were very different people. James Wentworth Day sort to capture the atmosphere of the Essex rivers and was a very outspoken fighter when it came to saving something he valued. Hervey Benham's writing was based on the fact that he thoroughly understood and cared for his native county. Hervey was a great man for helping people and was the unseen hand behind many of the schemes to keep alive the traditional way of life.

More recently John Leather, Hugh Perks and Keith Lovell have all dutifully recorded much of the past of these great rivers. There is far more written about the Colne and Blackwater because these rivers have a colourful story. Apart from yachting very little has been recorded about the Crouch and even less about the Roach and its islands.

The Essex estuaries and their vast marshlands have proved a difficult subject for artists to capture, but this land of barges against river walls has produced some really good photographers working in black and white. Here I have drawn on my collection of photographs by Douglas Went of Brightlingsea who worked between 1923-50s, but there were several others. John Tarlton used his camera to find the very soul of this English county. Fortunately the Essex coast tradition of good photography is very much alive in people such as Burnham's Colloryan and Maldon's own Den Phillps. However none of these would have produced any good work unless the subject held a magic which they could catch at the right moment.

For information I have tried to draw on the knowledge of people who have know these waters for a life time and often have family traditions to draw on as well. Indeed the whole pleasure of writing this book was that I was in touch with the interesting people of this coast.

Help came from many sources. Dick Harman, Malcolm Macgregor, John Cragie and James Lawrence guided me on the Colne. Bobby Stoker of West Mersea, who started skippering the smack *Mayflower* under sail about 1932, was happy to pass on his knowledge of old fishing ways. Also on Essex smacks Charles Harker, David Green and John Rowley helped. Rodney and Hilary Hucklesby helped with 'Down East' on Mersea, while Daphne Allen and came to the rescue with Fingringhoe and Bill Brown with Rowhedge. From Tollesbury Aubrey Heard and

Gayle Heard helped. While at Maldon Michael Emmett has a memory which seems to go back several generations. Brian Kennell has also cleared up several points about Maldon and the local smacks he knows so well. Patricia O'Driscoll remembered her time in barges and was keen to help and more expert knowledge came from Barry Pearce and Pat Fisher.

In 1960 we sailed *Sea Fever* to up to Battlebridge for the first time and I remember being surprised that such a long river, apart from Burnham, could be so empty of yachts. This has changed and I am grateful to the Royal Corinthian Yacht Club, Royal Burnham Yacht Club and Commander Twist of the Crouch Harbour Authority for bringing me up to date. On their Burnham boatyard information came from Murray and Robin Prior. Also on the Crouch Ron Pipe and Trevor Taylor have a fund of knowledge. On the Roach, the river pilot Mo Deal and Vivian Llewellyn have provided useful material and Tony Judd and Graham Wadeson have brought me up to date. Mike Todd talked about white weeding which he has taken part in since 1955. While Mick Wilkinson's wandering life style means that he has been part of many of the maritime events in Essex in recent decades.

The original research for this book required many pleasant days sailing, sometimes followed by peaceful nights at anchor, in these waters. More recently Pearl and I have walked in several areas in order to get to know the rivers from another angle. However the finished work calls for other skills. I thank Geoff Cordy for the photographic work, my daughter Caroline Southernwood and K. C. Lockwood for the illustrations and most of all my wife Pearl for the many hours spent editing and more important for tolerating my obsession for recording these estuaries.

R. S.
Ramsholt.

Source of illustrations

Martin Suirrell 4,5. John Dalzel 25. Jack Fuller 6,16. D. Went 2, 14, 15, 17, 18, 19, 20, 21, 23, 28, 30, 38, 49, 73, 80, 107. East Anglian Daily Times 64, 85. M. Jay 93. Tony Ellis 31, A.R.J. Frost 39, Daphen Allen 40, 41, 44, 50, 55 R. Hucklesby 42, 43. E & A.F. Tomblin 54. Essex County Standard 46, 47. John Tydeman 48. Evening Gazette 45. P. O'Driscoll 11A, 51, 94, 96, 101, 119, 122. Colchester Borough Council 52, 53. Jack Coote 56, 106, 121, 124, 128. John Tarlton 57, 105. A. Mahoney 58. M. Yardley 111. Royal Burnham Yacht Club 112, 113 R.J. Prior & Son 114, 115, 116, 117, 118. Janet Harber 123, 125, 126, 127.Vivian Llewellyn 130, 131, 132, 133. D.A. Lawrence 71.A. Heard 74.Eric Boesch 89, 95, 108. Barry Pearce 77A, 135A, 135B. Colin Fox 139. The rest from the author's collection or taken by him.

'Gladys' and 'May' beating to windward K. C. Lockwood

Thames Sailing Barge 'Centaur' K.C. Lockwood

Chapter One

RIVER STOUR AND THE WALTON BACKWATERS

1. Green Bros Brantham flour mill at the head of the tidal River Stour with their sailing barge *Orion*. Greens had three small sailing barges which brought imported wheat from London docks. The *Orion*, sold in 1939, was the last one.

2. Greens mill at Brantham before it was burnt down. Above Manningtree the River Stour divides into two channels. Both these channels were closed by the barrier in 1971 and the last boat to sail up to Flatford lock was Charlie Stock's *Shoal Waters*.

3. Jack Lucas racing his spritsail rigged duck gun punt at Manningtree in 1985. The duck punts were used in the winter for shooting duck with a large gun mounted on the bow. Some punt gunning still takes place on the River Stour, however the Lucas family have kept alive the Essex tradition of summer punt races.

4. Mr Bennett mending a shrimp net at Harwich in 1950. Shrimping was a summer fishery.

5. Four Tollesbury smacks at Harwich in 1950. The trawls were hauled aloft to dry because the cotton nets rotted quickly if left wet. These smacks were all built as sailing craft, but had motors fitted and sails removed. These four Tollesbury smacks would have either trawled in the Thames Estuary or in the autumn they went to Boston after sprat.

6. The holiday club on Stone Point at the entrance to Walton Backwaters in 1934. This club was very popular with yachtsmen because the police could not get out here to make sure the bar was closed on time. The club was burnt before World War II.

7. Walton Backwaters about 1911. In the centre is the Walton Channel with the Twizzle leading off to the left and the channel up to Walton goes to the right. Soil has been dug in the foreground to make up the river wall.

8. The Walton or Woodruffe tide mill at the head of the Foundry Reach in Walton Backwaters. The mill was driven by the water caught in a 30 acre pond. This tide mill was pulled down in 1921 and the windmill which stood beside it blew down the day the demolition was completed. The Walton and Frinton Yacht Club then built a club house on the site of the windmill. This club was originally the Walton Sailing Club, but in 1912 altered its name to yacht club.

9. Les Wall and Frank Bloom about to shoot an oyster dredge from the *Fox* in Walton Backwaters in 1969. Oyster rearing was started in Walton Backwaters by Mr and Mrs William Backhouse, who bred Arab horses on Horsey Island, Frank Bloom and Les Wall ran a summer pleasure boat off Walton-on-the -Naze beach. The first oysters froze to death by the severe winter of 1962, but the layings were restarted with wild European oysters from Cornwall. In 1995 Frank's son Owen Bloom was running the Walton oyster business.

10. The sailing barge *Mercy* alongside the Beaumont Quay about 1910. Before 1914 there was barge traffic into Walton, Kirby and Oakley. There was a large wooden warehouse on Landermere quay while a channel, Beaumont Cut, was specially dug to get barges to Beaumont Quay at the very head of the Backwater.

11. The Simper family sailing the *Pet* to Beaumont Quay in 1983. Most of the Victorian warehouses have been pulled down, but a tablet in the remaining building proudly proclaims that it was built with stone from the old London Bridge.

11A. Mistley shipright Mark Hicks using a draw knife on a mast in 1962. He was making a short derrick mast for Horlock's barge *Remercie* which was then having all the sailing gear removed so that she could trade as a motor barge.

Chapter Two

BRIGHTLINGSEA , PYEFLEET AND THE RIVER COLNE

12. People being evacuated from Jaywick after the 1953 Floods when 35 people were drowned in the town and two at Point Clear. Part of Jaywick was flooded again in 1987 when another tidal surge went over the top of the sea defences. Coastal Essex has always had to fight hard to keep the sea back. There have been people in each generation who have suggested abandoning coastal Essex. However in this heavily populated county there is a very real need to maintain all the sea defences to protect homes, land for food production, wild life habitat and open places of people to walk in. However the battle to get money and support to keep up sea defences has always been far greater than the technology needed to keep back the sea.

Above. 13. A tripper boat waiting for passengers at Clacton pier in about 1910.

Left. 14. The 93ft schooner *Tamesis* getting under way off Brightlingsea in about 1935. Even then this yacht which was built in 1875 was a ghost from the past. For over a century up to 1939 yachting had been a major employment in the Colneside villages. The men worked their smacks in the winter and became the professional crews on the yachts in the summer.

15. Brightlingsea in 1934. The sailing barge *Anglia*, then skippered and part owned in Brightlingsea by George Ventris is being hauled on to the Hard with a dolly line. On the right in the foreground is one of the oyster storage legends. While Colchester's bucket dredger is lying in front of Stone's yard.

So that the channel could be dredged for oysters the smacks at Brighlingsea creeks and Thornfleet, West Mersea had 'one legged moorings'. These moorings had one anchor at the side of the channel and when the smacks were sailed in anchors were dropped on the other side to form a mooring which could be removed.

The older part of Brightlingsea is around the High Street, but during the Victorian period the expansion of the oyster trade and the yachting brought shipbuilding to the town. Three new streets were laid out linking the High Street with the Waterside. Tower Street was known as 'Discount Street' because the yacht stewards and then captains bought there own houses here on the 'discounts' they got from seeing that orders were placed with Brightlingsea shipbuilders and tradesmen.

16. Smacks dredging for oysters in the Colne in 1935. The nearest smack was built as the *Foxhound*, but after rebuilding in 1914 she became the *TCHJ* .

The method used to take oysters off the bottom of the river was for the smacks to move slowly sideways, propelled mainly by the tide, dragging the dredges along the bottom. The heavy iron dredges had to be hauled back on deck by hand and then the contents sorted out. The four men on the *TCHJ* are each working one hand dredge. These company smacks worked under the direction of a foreman and at the end of the day he hoisted a flag to say when to sail for home.

17. The steam paddle oyster dredger *Pyefleet* bringing smackmen back to Brightlingsea from a days work over in Pyefleet in 1928. Colchester confirmed its ownership of the River Colne in 1189 by agreeing to help King Richard the Lionheart to pay for the repairs to Dover Castle. Brightlingsea managed to stay outside Colchester's control so that the oyster layings in the creek here were always worked by individual oystermen. In order to get a revenue from the river Colchester leased it to the Colne Fishery Company in which some oystermen had shares. During the Victorian period the returns from the fishery were very good and helped to keep Colchester's rates low, but there were endless disputes about how the fishery should be managed. The oyster industry in Essex estuaries reached a peak about 1890 when it gave employment to around 1500 men and boys.

18. Sprats being spread on a field at Brightlingsea in 1925. At that time around forty smacks from the Colne and Tollesbury were landing sprat at Brightlingsea and most of these were put into barrels for export. When the market was glutted the sprats were sold to farmers as manure.

19. One of Douglas Went's photographs taken aboard a tug being used as a Committee boat at the Brightlingsea Regatta in 1931. The Regatta was then a grand local event sponsored by local firms.

20. Two of Samuel West's ballast barges *Saxon* and *Gwynronald* dressed overall for the 1938 Brightlingsea Regatta. Both these large wooden barges were fitted with engines because of the difficulties of working into the narrow Ray Creek for shingle. The *Saxon* was at the Jetty in the Ray when the 1953 Flood swept her over a river wall where she stayed for a long time.

21. Yachts, a barge and water taxis at the Brightlingsea Regatta in 1929.

22. Ron Hall's Maldon based 73ft steam tug *Brent* in the Colne in 1981. She was built for the Ministry of War Transport in 1946.

23. The 20ft Norman Dallimore-designed Royal Burnham class racing in the Colne in about 1936. Most of this class raced from the Royal Burnham Yacht Club, but the ones based at Brightlingsea were known as the Pye Fleet class. Robert Stone of Brightlingsea designed the Colne one designs which became the popular half decked racers on the Colne and Blackwater.

Above. 24. Workers at Sail Craft Ltd at Brightlingsea in 1967 with Reg White sitting in the middle of the front row. About 1957 Rod MacAlpine Downie designed and sold catamarans with Reg White at Brightlingsea in a shed hired from Orton and Wenlock. This venture grew into Sail Craft which employed thirty-three people and built small racing catamarans and the cruising Iroquois class. In 1965 Reg White won the Little America Cup with the Downie designed *Emma Hamilton* and over the next decade dominated international catamaran racing. In 1976 Reg White won the Gold Medal at the Olympic Games at Toronto for catamaran racing.

Left. 25. A Sail Craft day boat catamaran Tornado class sailing in the Colne in about 1968.

26. George Peggs in his punt at Underwood's Hard just up the creek from Brightlingsea in 1896.

27. Looking across the mill pond to St Osyth tide mill. There was a mill on this site in 1491, but this mill was built in about 1730 and was last worked in 1929. It was blown down in 1962.

28. The Colne Oyster Fishery Packing shed in 1950. This was built on Peewit Island in Pyefleet in about 1888. The Packing shed was knocked down by the Floods in 1953 and replaced by a Nissen hut two years later. The wild European oyster from the Thames Estuary was proudly marketed as the Native oyster or sometimes Pyefleets although they were often brought here as young oysters from all over Britain. Oyster cultivation was highly secretive and led to endless friction which at times developed into little short of open war between rivals.

The Pyefleet is the eastern end of the channel running behind Mersea Island. It is a shallow creek, rich in plankton which makes it ideal for oysters. The Pyefleet was also a favourite anchorage for barges to come in and shelter in a south westerly blow. This led to conflict when they anchored on the oyster beds.

29. Aboard the company smack *Native* with an oyster skiff astern in about 1946. They appear to have finished dredging on the Binnaker off Brightlingsea which was then the only place where wild oysters bred in the Colne.

Oyster cultivation was very labour intensive with all the work being done by hand. Most of the river bed had to be kept covered in old shell and free from mud. Before the oysters were marketed at five years old they were constantly moved which included being brought ashore in the winter to be stored in pits on the saltings so that the ice did not kill them.

Although oysters generated employment there were far more smacks in Essex than the local fisheries could support so that they often went and raided other rivers. Between 1891-1942 the Colne fishery paid for the Colne River Police, which was part of the Colchester Borough Police Force. They patrolled the river in fast cutters. In the early days when the Colne police approached a smack suspected of poaching they did not put their hands on a rail as they came alongside. This invited the smackmen to put their boot on them.

30. Unloading oysters on Brightlingsea Hard about 1960. Oysters are being unloaded from one of the 21ft, nine planks aside, skiffs used for oystering. In the background is one of the Brightlingsea oyster storage 'legends' and beyond that a sail loft.

31. The Mayor of Colchester, Eric James', ceremonial hauling the first of the season's Pyefleet oysters on to the bawley *Helen & Violet* in 1982. The tradition was that after the first dredge has been hauled the mayor and his party took gin and ginger bread.

The falling numbers of oysters saw the Colne Fishery Company steadily decline so that after World War II only a few dredgermen remained. The very hard winter of 1963 killed almost all the Essex oysters. The Colne Fishery was abandoned for two years after this and then Christopher Kerrison took up the lease and formed the Colchester Oyster Fishery. This Company worked hard for many years to revived the oyster fishery until the oysters were hit by the disease Bonamia in 1982.

32. James Lawrence and Mark Butcher working on the mainsail of the barge *Centaur* in 1986 in their Brightlingsea sail loft. Jim Lawrence grew up at Colchester near the Hythe Quay and in 1948 when he was fifteen he went as third hand on the sailing barge *Gladys* and at eighteen was skipper of the *George Smeed*. After various jobs ashore and afloat he returned to barges to skipper the *Marjorie* for six summers from Maldon in the new holiday charter work. Looking for a winter occupation he started sail making and moved to Brightlingsea where he established James Lawrence, Sailmakers, in 1970. As well as building up a successful business he has been equally successful racing the bawley *Helen & Violet*. After this he had the smack *Lily May* and then the bawley *Saxonia*.

33. The spritsail barge *Mirosa*, one of several very attractive barges built by Howard at Maldon, and the stowboat (sprat) smack *ADC* leading their classes in the 1974 Colne Smack and Barge Races. In the Victorian times there were some 1300 smacks and barges registerd in the Colne and Blackwater. This was the golden age of sail on the Essex coast, but by the 1950s this massive fleet had become a collection of wornout wooden boats which where left to rot in creeks or sold as yachts. From the 1930s people were converting these former work boats into yachts, but in the early 1960s a strong revival movement started and owners began restoring craft to their traditional appearance, although they were still sailed for pleasure or holiday charter.

34. The clinker built bawley *Marigold* at the start of the 1984 Colne Smack and Barge Race. She is being sailed by David Patient who built her at Maldon in 1981. The carvel hulled bawley which sailed from Harwich, Southend and Leigh had a flat transom stern and loose footed mainsail. While the smack which sailed from the Colne, Blackwater, Crouch and Roach had the beautiful slopping counter stern and a boom at the foot of the gaff mainsail.

35. Start of the Colne Smack and Barge Race in 1985. Left to right *ADC*, *Charlotte Ellen*, *Peace*, *Saxonia* and *Helen & Violet* .

36. The Maldon smack *Fly* at the start of the 1990 Pyefleet Smack and Bawley Race. Most of the traditional revival movement was centred around racing so Chrisopher Kerrison of the Colchester Oyster Fishery held this race in which the boats had to either catch shrimp or dredge oysters under sail so that the old skills were kept alive.

37. Smacks racing around Rat Island in 1990. This must be the ultimate in flat Essex islands, just a patch of open saltings. However ways have to be found to save all this type of land from the encroaching sea.

Above. 38. Reed cutting at Thorrington Tide Mill. The mill was built on a foundation of elm trunks in 1831 and worked until 1926. Tom Glover then used the mill to store seeds in and because he loved mills restored it. In 1974 Glover sold the mill to the Essex County Council.

Right. 39. The brigantine *Cap Pilar* at Wivenhoe Shipbuilders in 1956. This wooden sailing vessel was built at St Malo in 1911 for the Grand Banks cod fishery but became famous after a group of adventurers sailed her on a voyage round the world between 1936-38. After many years of being laid up on the Colne she was towed to Cook's dry dock in 1969 where she was broken up.

40. Sailing barges at the Ballast Quay, Fingringhoe in the 1920s. The quay appears to have been first built in about 1840 and the two cottages on the quay were pulled down in the 1920s.

41. The Ballast trade from the Colne greatly increased after the conveyor belt was fitted in 1947. This was reputed to have been a mile long and cost £1 per foot. Before this, horse drawn rail trucks were used to get the ballast down to the quay for grading into sand, shingle and stone.

42. The ballastman *Bert Prior* near the SW Maplin during a force 9 gale in 1983. The ballastmen's routine is to run between the Fingringhoe pit and the Thames wharves about 3-4 times during a working week. The original Prior fleet was *Peter P*, *Sidney P*, *Colin P*, *Leonard P* and the *A. H. P* all ex-World War I Gallipoli landing craft. In 1994 the *Peter P* was still with the fleet and was the oldest British vessel to still hold a load line certificate. The others in the fleet then were the *Brenda P*, *James P*, *Bert Prior* and *Mark Prior*. The Prior family started as barge owners in 1870 and opened the ballast pit at Fingringhoe in 1934. Ballast is sorted into sand, shingle and stone before being shipped to London.

43. Loading 260 tonnes of shingle on to Prior's ballastman *Bert Prior* at Fingringhoe in 1991. On the right is skipper Rodney Hucklesby then mate Jim Graham and alongside is the *James P* with her mate Leslie Rouse.

44. The Drop. Because the nineteenth century square riggers in the coal and timber trades could not sail without a cargo they had to stop at Fingringhoe when outward bound and load ballast to keep them stable. The ballast came from a pit known as the Dingle. A World War II pill box is on the site of The Drop.

45. The launching of the Jubilee Trust's barque *Lord Nelson* from James Cook's shipyard at Wivenhoe in 1985. This was the last large vessel built in a Colne shipyard.

46. Wivenhoe ferry just before it was closed in 1956. There had been a ford across the river, but about 1847 Colchester Corporation wanted to get larger ships up to their port so they agreed that if they could dredge the river deeper they would operate a ferry 'for ever'. However the horse and coal carts continued to ford the river at low tide until about 1937. With the ford and ferry, Fingringhoe's Hyde Park Corner was virtually part of Wivenhoe with men going across to work and even the doctor coming across.

In 1955 Colchester wanted to close the ferry, but the Fingringhoe people protested, raised money and took their case before the Lord Chief Justice, Lord Goddard. Led by Chairman of the Parish Council Dorothy Cock and shipwright Derrick Allen, they hired a bus and went to London to fight their case in High Court. However Lord Goddard ruled that Colchester did not have to run a ferry.

47. The new Wivenhoe Ferry being opened in 1992 with eighty year old Dorothy Cock and Daphne Allen aboard, both had fought to keep the original ferry open thirty seven years before. After this the Regatta Committee used to run the ferry for one day. In 1992 the Wivenhoe Ferry Trust opened a new triangular service between Wivenhoe, Rowhedge and Fingringhoe on high tides during summer weekends.

48. The 286ft(88m) *Sea Weser* outward bound past Wivenhoe in 1990. At the time she was said to have been the longest ship to come up the Colne. Ships were getting larger and the Colne stayed the same size. This view is from the former 'Lord Nelson' public house where people used to call on their way to the Ferry over to Wivenhoe.

49. Looking from Wivenhoe church across to the Roman River or Fingringhoe Creek. The mill at the head of the creek started as a tide mill.

50. Looking down the Colne from Wivenhoe before the barrage was built.

51. Motor barge *Ethel May* waiting for wheat to be discharged at Fingringhoe Mill in 1960. The Colne pilot Guy Harding acted as huffler to take barges up the Roman River. Getting round the last bend before the mill was very difficult for a loaded barge. Barge traffic up here stopped in about 1972.

52. Looking from Wivenhoe up the Colne to Rowhedge in 1994. The villages of Wivenhoe and Rowhedge grew up at the first place where the river valley narrows. These two villages offer sheltered anchorages and an easy river crossings.

53. The motor vessel *Gama* unloading fertilizer at Rowhedge Quay, 1994. From the 1930s the Port of Colchester expanded by handling bulk dirty cargoes. It appears to have reached its peak during the Miner's Strike of 1984 when all the twenty berths in the river were occupied and there were about another eighteen coal ships waiting at anchor near Brightlingsea. All this century until 1989 the port had earnt money for its owners the Colchester Borough Council. After this the number of ships discharging here began to steadily fall. Colchester's main import, fertilizer for local farms, was hit by the world trade recession. However the main reason for the decline was that ships grew larger and went to ports such as Mistley and Ipswich which had deeper water.

54. Looking up the Colne past Ian Brown's yard at Rowhedge in the about 1984. The quay in the foreground is on Cat Island where Ian Brown replaced the old paint store with a new house. Next is the chandlery and behind that the covered slipway, one of three on the yard, where the RNLI lifeboats were repaired. Beyond that is the Brewery Wharf. Brown's built thirteen wooden yachts and then went over to a 'do it yourself' yard with lifeboat repair. When wooden hulled lifeboats dropped out of use the yard closed.

55. Rowhedge Ferry in the 1960s. There had also been a ford across the Colne at Rowhedge, but the flat bottomed ferry boat was used by shipyard workers until the ferry closed in 1968.

Above. 56. Stackie barges being towed away from Colchester in 1946. This brief revival of an old trade was to take straw to a paper mill in Kent. The barges are being towed down to Alboro Point by one of Colchester's two small motor boats. Before this men in harness towed barges down to Rowhedge using a light cotton rope.

Left. 57. Francis & Gilders' barge *Lady Helen* at the Hythe, Colchester in about 1950. When the Essex farm wharf trade started to die out in the early 1920s Josh Francis began to get all the Colne and Blackwater 'seeking' barges under his management and in 1933 the firm of Francis and Gilders was founded. This Colchester firm had fourteen sailing barges until after World War II when they began to sell the smaller ones and fit engines in the larger ones. Francis and Gilders merged with the London & Rochester Trading Company in 1951 and their barges *Kitty*, *Centaur*, *George Smeed* and *Mirosa* traded under sail until 1955 when they were sold to become timber lighters at Heybridge Basin.

58. *Dawn* up at East Mills, Colchester about 1954. In about 1850 the millers Marriage had the head of the Colne straighted so that sailing barges could get up here. In the 1890s Marriages owned the sailing barges *Fleur de Lis* and *Voilet*. In 1914 they had the *Leofleda* built by Cann at Harwich. She was named after the Anglo Saxon lady who had owned land in Colchester. The millers also chartered the smaller Francis and Gilders barges to bring up wheat. It was quite a trip to get up to East Mills as the mast had to be lowered and then the barge drifted up on the tide under three bridges. The mast had to be raised again to unload the freight.The *Leofleda* was sold in about 1954 and the *Mirosa* brought the last freight up here the following year. In 1983 the mill closed and was converted to a hotel. The *Raven* was berthed on the mill quay to add a little character to the setting, but was later abandoned just down the channel.

Chapter Three

WEST MERSEA, TOLLESBURY AND THEIR CREEKS

59. A party going out on the path over the saltings to the Essex Naturalist Trust's Ray Reserve in 1986. The Ray Reserve between the Strood and Ray Creek is 110 acres of which only 25 acres, Ray Island, is above the high tide line.

During the Victorian period Ray Island was let out for cattle and sheep grazing. There were hedges on the Ray dividing up the grazing and a pond with a small barn or even cottage near it. The Ray was then abandoned and only visited by wildfowlers and poachers. The trees grew up on The Ray and in 1970 the Essex Naturalist Trust bought the area. In 1985 they put sheep back on the island to improve the bird habitat, but these all vanished during a bad gale over Christmas. Later a small flock of Soay sheep survived on the Ray and kept down the grass.

Opposite Top. 60. The Packing Shed and oyster storage pit on Packing Marsh Island, West Mersea in 1973. This shed on a saltings island off West Mersea was completed in 1887. It was the headquarters of the Tollesbury and Mersea Native Fishery Company where oysters were packed into bags. Many oysters were exported in a ketch that came over from France to collect them. The shed was abandoned in the 1920s when the oyster fishery started to decline. About 1990 a trust was formed to preserve the Packing Shed.

Opposite Bottom. 61. The winkle brig *Mary Agnes* dredging for oysters. This 15ft open gaff boat was built by W.Cook & Son at Maldon in 1971. The open boats at Cooks were built by Alf Last in the shed which later became the Maldon Maritime Centre.

Until about 1914 Merseamen were using 20ft 'haul and towing' open boats for dredging oysters in the narrow creeks. These 'two ended' (pointed at both ends)boats were worked by two or more men between two anchors. The dredge was dropped overboard and the men hauled it along the bottom by winching the boat back to the opposite anchor.

Gaff rigged open boats were introduced to dredge under sail in the creeks. Because they carried heavy loads the brigs had grown frames. It required a good breeze to dredge with a sailing boat and they sometimes used a 2ft dredge instead of the normal 3ft. The term 'winkle brig' which was used at Mersea was a bit of local joke, because in about 1910 these miniature smacks were used to sail across to The Main off Bradwell to gather winkles. About fifteen Mersea winkle brigs were built by Kirby at Brightlingsea. In the 1930s heavy clinker oyster skiffs were built and fitted with engines, but some winkle brigs went dredging under sail. About 1966 'Snowball' Hewes was still occasionally dredging with the *Boy George* under sail. On the Colne fishermen also used open gaff boats which they called bumkins.

62. West Mersea Causeway in 1973 before the yacht mooring posts were placed in the Ray Channel.

63. Houseboats at West Mersea in 1973. The grand Victorian yachts were based at Tollesbury, Rowhedge, Wivenhoe and Brightlingsea, but after 1912 many became houseboats along the Blackwater. This proved to be a reservoir of historic craft and some such as the 95ft *Artemis* at West Mersea and the lifeboat *Alfred Corry* at Maldon have been taken away for restoration.

64. The start of the 1969 West Mersea Smack Race. *Gracie* CK 46, *William & Emily* (*Odd Times*), and *Iris* CK 67. The records show this race was held back to 1928, stopped during World War II, was revived again in 1947 and until 1951 some working smacks were taking part.

65. Smacks *Gracie*, *Boadicea* and *Mayflower* lying at Johnny Milgate's Yard, Peldon at the top of Ray Creek in 1984. In the distance is the clump of trees on Ray Island out in the saltings.

In 1920 the Mersea Shell Crushing Co moved their mill from the Firs, West Mersea to the top of Ray Creek. This mill crushed the slippery limpets, an imported pest found on oysters, to make chicken grit. The Shell Bungalow remained after the mill closed and in about 1968 Johnny Milgate, who raced the smack *Peace*, established a boatyard here.

66. Mike Frost on his smack *Boadicea* at Peldon in 1984. Behind him are 'tendels' he had made. These were the traditional baskets used by West Mersea fishermen.

Mike Frost led the way in preserving the Essex smacks. He bought the 30ft *Boadicea* in 1938 and kept her in working order while other smacks sold out of fishing were altered to yachts. He was also the first person to totally rebuild a work boat when he put the old *Boadicea* ashore at Tollesbury in the late 1960s and after a few years relaunched the new hull. After this other people began to follow suit.

The *Boadicea* was first launched at Maldon in 1808. She has the flat transom stern of the early nineteenth century. To get more deck space builders extended the decks to produce lute sterns. Not many lute stern smacks were built after 1860, although the *Mary*, *William & Mary* and *William & Emily* still existed in 1995. The yacht influence created the Victorian smack with its deep forefoot and long counter stern.

67. Early morning in the Quarters with *Gracie* and Charles Harker's *Iris* at the start of the 1971 West Mersea Smack Race. The working smacks used to have an annual race at each fishing village. These races died out in the interwar years as motors were fitted, but in 1947 the West Mersea race was started again.

68. The smack *Mary* rounding The Nass beacon at the start of the 1971 West Mersea Smack Race up to Maldon. The smack races retained the character of a village event sailed between men who knew each other well.

69. The smack *Shamrock* racing in the Blackwater in 1971. In Victorian times the term smack meant a decked gaff rigged fishing craft. Between 1780 and 1938 some 1600 sailing smacks were built in Essex. The leading building port was Brightlingsea. Some 320 were launched here of which the Aldous family built around 175. The 44ft *Shamrock* was built by Aldous about 1900 and restored after her working life had ended when she was sunk by the ice in 1963.

70. David Green sailing his smack *Gracie* in 1990 off Mersea Island. The *Gracie* is a good example of local smack being restored and staying in her home waters. Built at Wivenhoe as a pleasure boat to work off Clacton beach, then converted for oyster dredging for the Cults of West Mersea. She was then sold to Maldon but Vic Herbert brought her back to Mersea in 1947 and then David Green bought her for pleasure sailing in 1967. Although there was still a great deal of oyster cultivation at West Mersea in the 1950s only Peter French and Bobby Stoker were fishing from here. When Richard Haward began selling fish this triggered off the development of a very active inshore fleet so that by 1980 there were eight boats operating from West Mersea.

71. Drake's 18ft punt on a family outing in Woodrolfe Creek, Tollesbury opposite the Rickus in 1907. The punt started off with leeboards to help her sail, changed to a centreboard and then an engine. In 1995 the punt was still in Frank Drake's garden.

72. Captain Edward Heard of Tollesbury on the J Class yacht *Endeavour*. Ted Heard was one of the best known professional yacht masters and went across the Atlantic to try and win back the America Cup. On the return passage in 1937 the *Endeavour* broke loose from the tug in a hurrican. The fate of Captain Heard and his crew became national news and it was assumed they had been lost, but they had hoisted the sails and completed the passage. Ted Heard died in 1947, but the flair for racing lives on in his grandson, Tollesbury sail-maker Gayle Heard.

73. Wildfowler Bill 'Chips' Levett of Tollesbury in a gun punt. In early Victorian accounts of wildfowl there are mentions of flocks of duck and geese several miles long coming in over the east coast to spent the winter on the estuaries. To the old countrymen this was a rich harvest which was there for them to take. The oldest decoy, ponds in which the duck were trapped, was at Steeple on the Blackwater. This was dug in 1713 and in the first winter the sale of 7364 duck paid for its construction. Wildfowling with guns started about 1750 and the Buckel family of Maldon claim to have been the first to mount a muzzle loading gun on a punt in about 1800. In 1860 32 Essex gun punts under the direction of an 'admiral' moved slowly in on a flock of wildfowl of St Peter's Point and killed 704 duck in a single combined blast.

There were duck punts in most of the Essex fishing villages and in hard winters the fishermen used them to earn a modest income. Duck punts were gradually used more for sport shooting although by 1985 the lack of duck and the new era of conservation meant that only a few punts were kept at Heybridge.

74. The Tollesbury smack *Ethel* shortly after being built in 1909. One of the last wooden smacks built, she appears to have been an 18ton 44ft 'stow-boater' used for winter sprat fishing. The *Ethel* was built for Lewis Heard who owned her until 1912. His son, another Lewis, started as 'apprentice dredgeman' in 1908 and later he became skipper of the smack *My Alice* and trawled in the Thames Estuary in the summer and went for sprat in the winter. In the early 1960s the Thames Estuary was 'fished out' of sprat so that Lewis, then seventy years old, took the *My Alice* to Boston for the winter to 'pair fish', which was towing a net between two smacks, for sprat.

75. Charlie Spooner's smack *Iris Mary* hauled up on Drake's slipway at Tollesbury in 1983. In the 1930s there were sixteen smacks fishing from Tollesbury, but by the 1950s only seven motorised smacks remained. Because they only worked in the sheltered Essex waters some of the wooden smacks had very long careers. The *Our Boys* was dredging oysters under sail from Mersea until 1947 and as a motor craft until the early 1980s. The *Iris Mary* was dredging oysters in the Blackwater until about 1985 which ended full time oyster work at Tollesbury. However in 1995 Trevor 'Mousey' Green had reopened two layings and Rigby's boat was fishing professionally in the winter.

76. The sail lofts at Tollesbury in 1971. The lofts were built in 1908 as winter storage for the gear from the large yachts which returned to lay up in the creek. During the summer many of the Tollesbury men went away as paid crews on the large yachts and in the autumn they brought the yachts back, laid them up and returned to their role as fishermen.

77. The start of Tollesbury Marina in 1971. The Drake boatyard was bought by John Goldie and Jack Waterhouse who had Tollesbury Marina dug and the first water was let in on a neap tide in 1970. Over the next twenty years the extra water flowing in the creek increased the depth, but possibly lead to silting in the South channel and Tollesbury Creek bar.

77A. Looking towards the mainland across the Strood from West Mersea in about 1910. Ragstone from the Medway is being discharged from a sailing barge for river wall repairs.

77B. Ted Woolf's roadside oyster sale room at West Mersea in 1975. This had its own oyster storage pits and was one of five purifying plants along the Mersea water front between The Lane and the 'Victory'. They were Banks, Mussett, Woolf, T&M Co and Peter French. Hervey Benham said that when Ted Woolf's oyster business closed in 1986 Mersea lost its most charming waterside feature.

THE RIVER COLNE, MERSEA ISLAND AND THE TOLLESBURY CREEKS

1. The Leavings. Where the sailing fishing smacks were anchored while their crews went ashore.

2. The Rickus. A path from Frost and Drake's across to where the Fellowship Afloat's light vessel is berthed was made by smackmen so that they could reach the deep water at low tide. The Chatterson's Path continues on across to Chatterson and Bowles Creeks which were named after oystermen.

3. Woodrope Hard, pronounced 'Woodup'. Drake's started at Old Hall Creek in 1835, but in 1850 they moved to the deserted Woodrolfe Creek and built the granary and shingle was brought in to make the hard. In 1904 Will Frost altered the granary from an Essex fly-hip roof to a gable ended one. Tollesbury owned barges brought in coal and took away sprat in barrels. The last barge with coal was Will Frost's *Mary Kate* which came in 1921.

4. Frost and Drake boatyard was an off shoot of the original Drake boatyard. The wooden loft here was originally Gowen's sail loft on the other side of the river wall, but when the new houses were built in 1972 Trevor 'Mousey' Green moved it over on to the the creek side.

5. In 1751 the top of Tollesbury Fleet was walled off to provide grazing marshes. In 1995 English Nature flooded these marshes to create s-altings for brent geese. It was also an expensive experiment for researchers to study how saltings are created.

6. Old Hall Marshes. In the 1890s 2000 sheep grazed on the marshes and the saltings outside the river wall. The Marsh is surrounded by 9 kilometres of river wall, was once famous as a wild fowling area until bought by the RSPB.

7. Old Hall Creek had in the mid-nineteenth century about fifty people living there and its own pub, 'Hoy Inn'. Coal for household fires, flint for the road and chalk to be burnt in lime kilns were brought in and hay, straw and mangolds were shipped out, but by the 1890s the trade had shifted to Woodrolfe Creek.

8. Salcott Creek. Sailing barges until around 1920 went right up to the Church and a few up to the 'White Hart' before the head of the creek was walled off.

9. In 1995 permission was given to a land owner on Salcott Creek to flood marshes to create habitat for wading birds, but this caused a loss of habitat for other marshland birds. The last place in Essex the authorities made a large capital outlay to save farm land was on Feldy Marshes in 1972.

10. On West Mersea water front Hempstead & Co built open boats from the 1920s until Clarke and Carter took over. West Mersea Yacht Club was founded in 1899 and became the leading yacht racing club on the Blackwater and Colne. The club originally used the houseboat *Molliette* and in 1934 moved to the club house. William Wyatt followed his father repairing smacks and building duck punts in his thatch and tiled shed near the Hard. 'Admiral' Wyatt died in 1961 aged 96.

11. Company Shed was built in about 1955 as an oyster cleaning plant and new headquarters for the T & M Company. About 1989 converted to a fresh fish shop by Heather Haward. There have been Hawards in the Mersea oyster industry since at least 1791.

12. Hulk of the skillinger *Pioneer*. The term 'skillinger' came from the Dutch island of Terschelling because these 80ft Brightlingsea smacks which had wet wells dredged oysters here and in the English Channel. The last skillinger *Fiona* sailed in 1931. By this time *Pioneer* was a house boat. She was moved to West Mersea in about 1945 and then abandoned.

13. The Strood. The origin of the causeway linking Mersea Island to the rest of Essex was discovered when a water main was laid across in 1978. It was found that the Anglo-Saxons had constructed the Strood around 690 by laying some 40000 oak trees across. On the mainland easterm side a short lived tide mill was built in 1734. Later, on the west side a barge quay used by stackies and by Wakeley's barges which brought in stone for the river walls until about 1947. Waterskiiers began to use this area in the late 1960s.

14. Wreck of the ferro-cement 125ft motor schooner *Molliette*. This was a cargo vessel built at Faversham in 1917 during the war time timber shortage and sunk here for bomber practices during World War II. The channel between the *Molliette* beacon and the Cocum Hills linking the Colne and the Blackwater was known as the Slog to smackmen.

15. Site of the East Mersea blockhouse. Built in 1540 to defend the Colne when England was at war with the French the blockhouse was seized during the Civil War in 1648 by the Parliamentary dragoons so that they could prevent ships going up to relieve Royalist forces trapped in the siege of Colchester.

16. Ferry across to Brightlingsea was run by E. Mole of East Mersea for 58 years. He died around 1938.

17. Wreck of the steamer *Lowlands*. The 260ft 1789 ton *Lowlands* was torpedoed near the North Foreland in 1916, but because she was loaded with timber tugs managed to get her into the Colne where she was abandoned after the cargo was removed.

18. Near North Farm there were three landing hards used by the fishermen when East Mersea was a plough and sail community. Last working smacks here until about 1939 were the *Daisy Belle* and *Meha-lah*. Colchester Oyster Fishery built a French style head quarters at North Farm in 1978.

19. Broad Fleet was dammed after the 1953 floods.

20. Ancient ford which was possibly the Roman route to Mersea Island. Along the original high tide line Red Hills are found along the Colne and Blackwater which seem to have been pre Roman salt making sites.

21. Geedon Creek. About 1900 there were cockle beds at the head of the creek and oyster beds lower down. The saltings were purchased in 1905 by the War Department and became the Fingringhoe Firing Range. The area here and the Langenhoe Marshes are to be avoided when the red flags are flying.

22. An early Roman wooden fort AD43-60. In the nineteenth century Wick Farm and Geedon saltings were mainly used for sheep grazing. About 1921 gravel pits started. Later Goldsmiths started the Fresh-water Sand & Ballast Co pit here and their barges loaded at The Jetty for Thames wharves. The pits closed when they ran out of land in 1961. Sold to Essex Wildlife Trust and became the 126 acre Fingringhoe Wick Nature Reserve.

23. Former jetty used for loading ballast barges. In 1979 J.Swine gave Jetty Hide for watching wading birds.

24. Ballast Quay first built in 1708 to supply ballast to sailing ships.

25. NRA Colne Barrier. First used in November 1993 to prevent the upper reaches from flooding.

26. In 1914 the Royal Engineers erected a bridge across the Colne at Rowhedge. This was very unpopular with bargemen but local people protested when it was removed. Rowhedge Wharf, below the village, replaced the ballast jetty built in the 1930s.

27. Cat Island Quay was formed about 1895 where Harris dug a slipway here and replaced a windlass with a steam winch.

28. Lower Yard, Rowhedge was where the Rowhedge Iron Works built wooden boats. In the early 1860s Phillip Mosely Sainty built a 200 ton barque here. Then called the Down Street Yard.

29. Upper Yard, Rowhedge. In 1830s called the Up Street Yard. Sailing and steam yachts built here in the 1870-80s by W.Puxley. About 1890 John Houston took over and built large yachts here. The firm of Rowhedge Iron Works took over in 1904. Later it was their Upper Yard building steel steamers and many were shipped in pieces all over the world. In 1963 the 200ft tanker *Mahtab* was the largest vessel ever launched at Rowhedge. Yard closed in 1963 by which time 947 vessels had been built here.

30. Mill Creek. In the early 1900s the large yachts were laid up here for the winter.

31. The channel on this bend switches to the 'wrong side' because above here the channel is not a natural one and was dredged out after 1860. In the medieval period the ships had grown too large to get above Wivenhoe and cargoes were transhipped to barges which were towed up.

32. Haven Quay and King Edward Quay. In the mid-1980s the Colchester Quays were very busy, but then the average ship was 50-60m long and loaded about 1000 tons, but as ships rapidly grew larger these quays were used less.

33. Swinging berth. Just below in 1740 a lock was built here to try and improve the port, but it was not successful. In the early 1970s when Colchester was booming as many as eight ships followed each other up on a tide. Up coming ships went straight on to the outside of their berth and the ship which had discharged slid out stern first and then went up to take her turn in the swinging berth. In 1995 a new road crossed the empty quays and river here.

34. The Hythe. Probable site of the medieval port of Colchester. Sheepen up above East Mills was a late Iron Age and early Roman industrial site and the possible site of the Roman port.

35. Phillip Sainty, builder of the famous yacht *Pearl*, took over the shipyard at the north end of Wivenhoe in 1831. He was followed by Thomas Harvey building mechants ships, smacks and yachts. His son John Harvey followed him mostly building large yachts and until the yard was forced to close in 1881. In 1888 Forrestt reopened the yard followed by Rennie. In 1930 the yard was closed and a forty year embargo placed on it, but it was reopened as Wivenhoe Shipyard in World War II. Reputed to have been 500 shipbuilders working in Wivenhoe building minesweepers and naval craft. Slipways were constructed above the Railway Quay to build craft for the D-Day Normandy Invasion. Wivenhoe Shipyard closed in 1962. Wivenhoe Wharf was built as a timber importing wharf about 1969. Later used for small bulk carriers and enjoyed a boom period during the 1980s. Last freight here in 1990 after which the site was sold for housing.

36. North Sea Canning Co. Canning sprat here 1932-60. Had their own boats and others fished on contract.

37. Wivenhoe water front badly shaken in 1884 earthquake. The Rosabelle Shed was put up to store the gear from the 450 ton steam yacht *Rosabelle*. Guy Mannering's Colne Marine & Yacht Co in the water front buildings. Wooden yachts built until 1967. Largest was the 46ft *Ylva* in 1958.

38. Marriage's Bight. The milling family of Marriage lived in the big house above the river.

39. River walls around Alresford Creek put up about 1730. When the 'whelk and winkle' railway line from Wivenhoe to Brightlingsea was laid a swing bridge was put across the creek to allow craft in. Bridge demolished in 1967. Until 1914 stackie barges loaded on the Ford and at five places between here and Thorrington Tide Mill. In 1932 sailing barges started to load ballast from the 'sand works' jetty. Originally they poled themselves, but after World War II a motor boat towed them in. The Alresford pit switched to mainly road transport in 1958, but a few barges for ten years after this.

40. The little dock at the Thorrington Tide Mill held two sailing barges and was used until about 1926. Bricks from Thorrington brickfield were also loaded here. About 1900 the St Osyth barge *Lucretia* came into Alresford Creek about five times a year to load a freight of 30000 bricks from Husk and Harper brickyard.

41. Bateman's Tower. Built about 1880 by squire John Bateman on the West Marsh. Used in the summer by his family and friends as bathing hut, but main purpose was in the winter as retreat for wildfowlers caught on the open marshes. In 1974 the Tendring District Council wanted to pull the tower down because it was leaning, but local protest prevented this. When the bathing huts were built Navvies Creek on the bend was dammed up to form the swimming pool.

42. Ancient ferry between Brightlingsea Waterside and St Osyth's Stone. In the 1930s forty-five men worked water taxis in the summer taking people who had arrived by railway over to the beach huts on St Osyth or across to East Mersea. After World War II fifteen men worked rowing ferries. They were not allowed to use motor boats. In 1994 ferryman Dick King and one water taxis operated at Brightlingsea.

43. Although there were some large mooring buoys for fishing boats in the South Channel until 1939 most smacks just anchored in Brightlingsea Creek. The Royal Navy put in mooring buoys further up the South Channel for yachts after World War II. These were replaced by posts in about 1974.

44. Douglas Stone opened a shipyard here in 1892 and built yachts. John James was building smacks next to Brightlingsea Hard and the two yards merged into James & Stone in 1924. When the yard closed in 1987 sixty-five people lost their jobs. This was one of five shipyards between Rowhedge and Brightlingsea which had provided three hundred jobs to the area.

45. Aldous Heritage Dock. formerly a slip here was part of the Aldous shipyard. About 1976 local smack owners rented the dock so that they could have a place to keep local traditional boats.

46. Formerly Aldous shipyard. This is probably where Philip Sainty had a yard building smuggling craft, yachts and smacks before he moved to The Hythe, Colchester about 1800. Matthew Warren building here until James Aldous took over in 1833. Aldous yard built fishing smacks continually although by the 1880s it was also producing large yachts. In 1932 the yard became Aldous Successors specializing in building tugs, dredgers and small commercial craft which were shipped abroad and re-erected. The hanger sheds went up during World War II when Aldous were building Motor Torpedo Boats. The Aldous yard, which had four slipways closed in 1962. Inspite of strong local 'No Wharf' opposition a new quay was built over the shipyard in about 1983. Further protests to try and close the wharf over wheat exports and again when Polish coal came in during the Miner's Strike. 1995 local BALE joined with animal rights protesters to try and force the end of exports of live animals in the *Caroline* to Niewpoort. Many Brightlingsea people resented the disturbances at the dock gate.

47. Underwood's Hard named after oysterman who owned part of the creek bed and saltings here. There was a cottage surrounded by its own sea wall out on the saltings until it was pulled down in 1937. Also a hard where sailing barges came for repair, but this and the cottage site are buried under the in fill around present quays.

48. Old name for Brighlingsea Creek was Borefleet. The old English word 'fleet' meant shallow. After the marshes were walled off the fleets were the fresh part of the old channel and the tidal channels were called creeks.

49 . The Folly. On Cindery Island a channel cut in about 1870 has steadily grown larger. The hulk of the Lowestoft steam drifter *Reality* here which was bought to fish out of Brightlingsea.

50. In the sailing barge era there were three farm wharves at the head of Flag Creek. The wooden jetty was used until 1939 when the ballast pit ran out. The over head bucket travelling line which came across the road was moved to Alresford.

51. Martin's Farm ballast jetty opened about 1961. In the 1980s five barges working here regularly. Routine was to make three trips to London every two weeks. Early 1990s less trade as London construction slowed down.

52. On the first bend on St Osyth Creek a small dock was dug in about 1932 for a sand pit which proved unsuccessful. The hulk of the stackie barge *Bluebell* was left here in about 1980.

53. Osyth locally pronounced 'Toosey'. St Osyth's Tide Mill barge dock had a low 'half tide' quay so that the carts could back up to barges at deck level. Maltings burnt down in 1920. In the 1930 slump twenty two sailing barges were laid up at the head of the creek. Developed as a boatyard in 1946 to convert five MTBs to houseboats during the housing shortage. Later the quay made higher and extended. Boatyard run by Andy Harman from 1987.

54. Ray Creek. From about 1930-57 Samuel West's barges were loading shingle brought from the Point on a narrow gauge railway to the Barge Pier in Ray Creek. The shingle went to Queenborough for glass making. Also a drag line loaded barges on the open Colne beach. Barges were hauled off the beach sideways to a single anchor. After this some 400 acres of Colne Point became an Essex Naturalist's Trust reserve for brent geese, sanderlings, curlew, redshanks and little tern.

55. Lee-over-Sands. In 1932 a company started to develop a holiday resort here. This had its own golf course and air strip, but the project failed and the flat rooved houses were left on stilts beside Horse Wash Creek. In the 1953 Floods only the marshman Macgregor and his family were living in Lee-over Sands and they rowed to Wick Farm. The marshes had been very good cattle grazing, but after the expense of repairing the river walls the government encouraged all marshes to be ploughed up. In 1995 about a dozen people were living in the houses on stilts and the Essex Wildlife Trust had taken over the Reserve. The warden said he was fighting a loosing battle to keep people and their dogs from destroying the little terns nests.

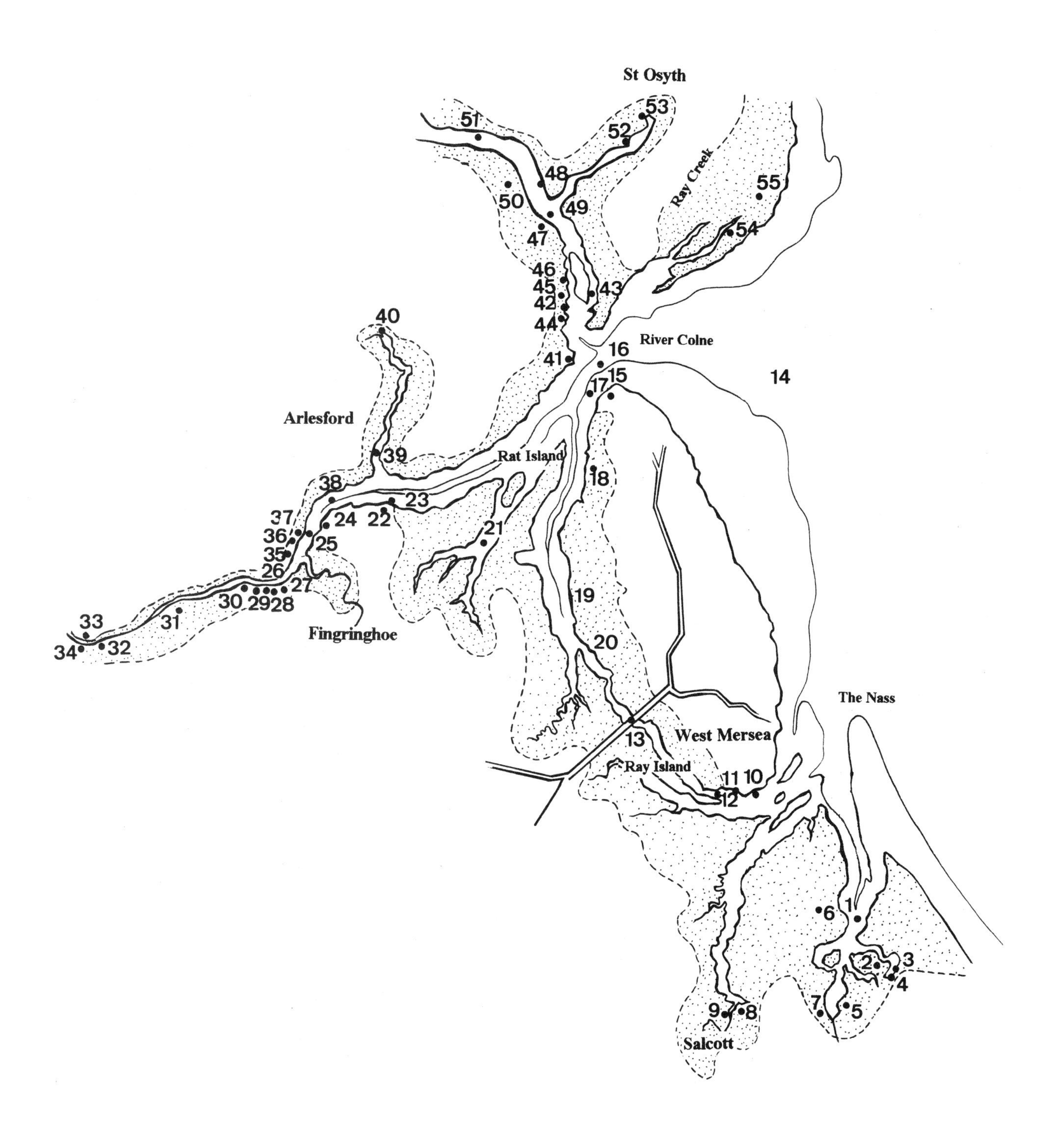
St Osyth
Ray Creek
River Colne
Arlesford
Rat Island
Fingringhoe
West Mersea
Ray Island
The Nass
Salcott
1
2
3
4
5
6
7
8
9
10
11
12
13
14
15
16
17
18
19
20
21
22
23
24
25
26
27
28
29
30
31
32
33
34
35
36
37
38
39
40
41
42
43
44
45
46
47
48
49
50
51
52
53
54
55

Chapter Four

THE WIDE RIVER BLACKWATER

78. The Mistley built steel barges *Reminder* and *Xylonite* beating up to the Wallet Spitway Buoy in 1985 Colne Race. Once they earnt their living carrying grain from London to Mistley, but this was replaced by taking passengers from Maldon.

79. Dick Norris' smack *Stormy Petrel* and Jon Wainwright's *Deva* near the Buxey Buoy in the 1986 Old Gaffers Race.

The East Coast Old Gaffers Race started in 1963 with a race from Osea Island to Harwich, but it was not really a popular event until it started and finished at the Stone Sailing Club. The Old Gaffers Association was started as a reaction against mass produced boats and fibre glass hulls. There was also great pressure at that time to stamp out the gaff rig and completely replace it with the bermudian rig. The Old Gaffers Association was formed to bring back respectability for wooden gaff boats by providing events which owners could take part in.

80. Walter Linnett, last of the Essex professsional wildfowlers, in his punt on the saltings out side his cottage at Bradwell in 1939. Although he made a living from taking wildfowl he once told a duck shooter 'if you have got a pound in your pocket boy, you don't need to kill the duck'.

This photograph was taken by Douglas Went and used by James Wentworth Day who wrote on country subjects. Wentworth Day saw Linnett as a symbol of the old order in which men made a living by working the land and harvesting the sea. He was well aware of the two influences on the Essex coast, the quiet traditional way of life and the Londoners moving out to impose colonies of cheerful brash houses in this rural landscape.

81. The chapel of St Peter's on the Wall at Bradwell in 1992. In 654 Bishop Cedd was sent here by the King of the East Saxons to build a chapel in the ruins of the Roman fort of Othona. The early Christians believed that the further you were away from people the nearer you were to god. St Peter's on the Wall is one of the oldest churches in Britain and its name refers to the miles of sea wall which reaches from Bradwell to Burnham. Past generations were impressed with the great determination it had taken to create this long wall by hand.

82. The brigantine *Sey Pirate* and barge *Reminder* anchored in St Lawrence Bay in 1986. The *Sey Pirate* was a Dutch fishing vessel converted to a brigantine at Cooks yard. The *Reminder* celebrated 25 years of charter work from Maldon in 1995.

83. Harvest on Osea Island in 1903. The island farm of Osea is linked to the mainland by a causeway and is only accessible at low tide. Because it is remote F.N.Carrington bought Osea in 1903 and turned it into a home for alcoholics. Some of the Maldon fishermen had a sideline smuggling alcohol down to Osea. However curiosity about Osea brought trippers to Maldon and the small steamer *Annie* ran trips down the river so that people could see the home.

84. The cottages on Osea about 1909. The mansion house was built about 1910 by F.N. Charrington. In 1916 Osea became a Royal Navy secret base for motor torpedo boats. The island remained a naval establishement until 1926.

85. The Thames barges *Mirosa*, *Marjorie* and *Kitty* at the start of the 1967 Blackwater Sailing Barge Match. On the left is the Maldon pleasure boat *Viking Saga*. After the Maldon race was restarted in 1962 it triggered off tremendous enthusiasm for keeping traditional craft sailing.

86. Gordon Swift at the wheel of the Maldon barge *Dawn* in 1986 with his son Gerard on the right on the leeboard winch. The *Dawn* was built for the stackie trade and collected freights from farmers between the River Deben and Dover for delivery to the London wharves. Gordon Swift bought the *Dawn* after she had been one of Brown's unrigged timber lighters at Heybridge and by 1966 she was back under sail.

87. The smack *Ostrea Rose* sailing on the Blackwater in 1983. This wooden smack was built in 1980 by Arthur Holt Ltd at Heybridge Basin for Michael Emmett. In design she is a throw back to the kind of smack that Michael's ancestors used when they moved in the Victorian times from the Thames to fish from Maldon. To start with *Ostrea Rose* dredged oysters under power on Michael's layings in Lawling Creek, but after oyster disease stopped the Blackwater fishery in 1983 he used her for charter from Hythe Quay.

88. Heybridge Basin, off Colliers Reach, at the entrance of the Chelmer and Blackwater Navigation in 1937 before ballast digging removed the marshes behind Herring's Point. The original idea was to build a canal from Maldon to take goods to Chelmsford, but the Maldon merchants stopped this so that they did not loose income from goods going over their quays. However the canal promoters overcame this by building a canal which joined the river at Heybridge thus insuring coal from the north of England could be taken up to Chelmsford far cheaper.

89. Heybridge Basin at the river end of the Chelmer and Blackwater Navigation in about 1960. Originally timber ships came into Heybridge Basin and then the timber was taken in 30 ton horse drawn barges up to 13 miles to Chelmsford. Then larger ships anchored off Osea Island and timber was off loaded into lighters and brought up to the Basin. The lighters were once towed up to the Basin, or Sadd's at Heybridge Creek, by a 35ft sailing tug. In 1965 the Basin lock was altered so that the Baltic ships could come in. At the same time five new canal barges powered by diesel outboards were purchased so that Brown's timber could be loaded directly into them. The last timber ship, the Danish *Conland*, discharged at Heybridge in 1971.

90. The bawleys *Marigold* and *Lilian* on the Bath Wall beach, Maldon in 1983. This beach was the home of Maldon's fleet of inshore fishing boats. The smacks either went trawling in the Blackwater mouth or for eels and oysters in the river. Through the effects of pollution in the Blackwater and general over fishing, stocks declined so that there was no capital to build new boats. In 1947 Hervey Benham recorded fourteen smacks at Maldon, all fully rigged, but most also fitted with old car engines. The last one trawling under sail only from Maldon or anywhere else for that matter was Ernie Pitt's *Polly* which he sold in 1956. He was then over eighty and had worked on this smack for seventy years.

91. Sailing barges at Maldon in about 1900. The nearest barge is at Walter Cook's yard while the others are lying on the Hythe Quay. Maldon was then the centre of the stackie trade. The horses on the streets of London and cows kept in barns to provide fresh milk created a tremendous demand for animal feed and litter. The flat bottomed spritsail rigged barges were ideal for this work because they could get into the shallow Essex creeks. They loaded mangolds in the hold and straw or hay on deck stacked half way up their masts. The stackie trade was at its height between 1860-1914 when there were fifty-six Blackwater barges, but once the trade dropped off numbers fell to seventeen in 1933.

92. Maldon about 1960. Greens Flour Mill at Maldon once owned two spritty barges *Ethel Maud* and the *May Flower*. In 1950 the *May Flower* became a yacht. In the distance, against the Hythe are barges converted to yachts and one still trading, but fitted with motors.

Above. 93. This is a classic view from St Mary's church tower Maldon. In the foreground is Walter Cook's yard with the barge *Dawn* under construction. She was launched in 1897. Maldon is a typical barge port because it dries out at low tide. Events such as the annual Maldon Regatta taking place here can only be held around high water.

Left. 94. Shipwright Cecil Wright of Cooks reshaping the *Ethel Maud's* mainmast with an adze in 1960 when she was 'converted to a motor barge'.

95. Walter Cook & Son's barge repair yard and the Hythe about 1962. Maldon, an old world port with the barge yards and sailmakers still operating, attracted people to bring their barges to Hythe Quay. The water front here became the centre of the traditional boat restoration movement with owners trying to keep their craft in working appearance.

96. At Cook's yard in 1968 a new fore hatch coaming is being put aboard the barge *Alice May*. Left to right John Pitt, John Fairbrother, Barry Peace, Alf Last and the skipper owner Arthur Jemmett.

97. Barges *Reminder* and *Wyvenhoe* being towed back to Maldon after the 1988 barge match. This was the most dramatic race after the matches were restarted in 1962. After starting off Osea and racing down river the barges turned to find themselves beating into a full south westerly gale. The barges were well handled and in good order and remarkably no serious damage was done. There were minor incidents such as the *Reminder* here had a bent sprit.

98. The *Victor* and *Gladys* returning to the Hythe after the 1993 barge match. Taking people on 'charter' trips was started at Maldon in the early 1960s as a way of getting an income to pay for barge maintenance. Within a few years the *Dawn*, *Kitty*, *Lord Roberts*, *Marjorie*, *Lady Gwynfred* and *Centaur* were in charter work. Often on a Sunday they returned up river together. All these barges had been fitted with engines except John Fairbrother's *Kitty*. John had been skipper of some the last barges trading under sail and brought the *Kitty* to the Hythe under sail.

99. In 1995 the charter barge *Thistle* bound down river while the smack *Joseph T* is lying on the Bath Wall. Doug Scurry with his *Joseph T* has kept alive the tradition of keeping Maldon smacks here.

100. The sail loft at Maldon in about 1914. In the foreground Arthur Taylor is measuring up while Bill Raven on the left and one of the Keeble family, on the right, are hand sewing the sails. In the centre is Joseph Sadler who had started this sail making business at Heybridge but moved up to the loft beside Howards yard about 1870. This loft had been converted from a granary by Gowen. Arthur Taylor bought the business in about 1914 and his son, Fred Taylor continued to run it until 1969.

101. Reg Barr who took Bill Raven's place at work in Taylor's sail loft in 1959. Reg had a two hour bus journey from his home at Brightlingsea every day, leaving at 7am and returning at 7pm.

102. Hervey Benham at the launch of his book on smugglers at Maldon Maritime Centre in 1986. Hervey Benham lived at West Mersea and had followed his grandfather and father as Editor of the *Essex County Standard.* He thoroughly understood the Essex coast and skilfully put across this understanding in his books. His early books, such as *Down Tops'l,* were the fuel which created the traditional boat revival movement.

103. Jamie Clay and Brian Kennell replanking the 47ft smack *My Alice* at the Downes Road boatyard in 1995. The planks have to be steamed in a chest to make them pliable and then quickly bent into shape on the frames. The main work was in the preparation and it was taking a week for three shipwrights to shape and fasten a plank on either side.

104. Brian Kennell working on rebuilding Jim Dine's *My Alice* at the Downes Road yard. The *My Alice* was built by Kirby at Brightlingsea as a Tollesbury stowboater in 1908 and finished as a power craft oyster dredging at Paglesham about 1985. The term rebuilding is a little misleading because the old hull was taken to pieces for patterns and a new hull constructed. Before this in, 1989 Richard Titchener's 44ft *Sallie* was also totally rebuilt at the Downes Road yard. She was built by Aldous in Brightlingsea in 1907 and was rescued from a rubbish tip in Whitby in 1980.

105. Maldon Crystal Salt Company. Salt being shovelled into drainage bins in 1983 and below C.B.Osborne skimming the surface of the steaming brine in one of the salt pans in 1964. The Blackwater is a very salty river because of the vast area of saltings and mud ooze. During the summer evaporation leaves a high salt content on the saltings which on a spring tide is swept up to Maldon where it is trapped in ponds before being boiled to produce the popular crystal salt.

Taking salt from the Blackwater is a very ancient industry dating back to well before Roman times. There were several salt works at Maldon when the Doomesday Book was compiled and by 1894 the Maldon salt works was the only sea salt factory left in Britain.

106. Auxiliary barge at Hasler's Wharf just below Fullbridge, Maldon in about 1954. The last sailing barge owned at Maldon was Green's *Ethel Maud* which Howard built in 1889. In 1995 the maximum size ship which came up to Green's Flour Mill on a spring tide was 550 tons with north American wheat. While Farm Supply on the wharf near Fullbridge had fish meal and wheat delivered for Greens.

Left. 107. Heybridge Mill was on the old course of the Blackwater. This mill worked until 1942 and was pulled down in about 1955.

Below. 108. Looking down the River Chelmer towards the railway bridge and Maldon about 1966. The railway reached Maldon in 1848, but the branch over the river was not built until 1888. The railway to Maldon closed in 1966, by which time road traffic had replaced the need for a railway.

109. The main Beeleigh Weir and Beeleigh upper lock in the Chelmer and Blackwater Navigation in about 1910. Originally the fresh water Chelmer and Blackwater joined the tidal estuary near Beeleigh Abbey. A weir was built to divert water to Beeleigh water mill which was burnt down in 1879. Before this barges, towed by tracking horses used to trade up to the mill. There was trade up the fresh water rivers long before the Navigation. Away inland on the River Pant above Braintree it was the practice, until about 1830, for men to move corn in small boats.

110. The main Beeleigh Weir about 1912 where the fresh water Blackwater crosses the Chelmer navigation to join the tidal estuary. Just below the Beeleigh lower lock the short Langford Cut runs up to Langford Mill. This Cut had barge traffic until 1881, while the main Navigation carried barge traffic between 1797-1972. The Navigation survived because it was not bought up and closed by a railway company. It escaped nationalisation and has always been an independent company.

110A. The *Irene*, the last of the West Country trading ketches, arriving at 'Maldon 1995'. As the *Irene* draws 9ft of water the fire brigade had to wash some of the silt away from Hythe quay to allow her to come along side. The year before a large traditional boat and shanty festival had been held and this led to the forming of the Maldon Town Regatta Association in the 'Queen's Head' to make it an annual event.

There were barge races held at Maldon before 1914 and another series took place between 1921–36. In 1962 twenty-one people met in the back bar of the 'Jolly Sailor', all put in five shillings and started the Blackwater Sailing Barge Match with *Marjorie* winning the first race up to the end of the Promenade.

RIVER BLACKWATER

1. A Bombing Range was established on the Dengie Flats in 1938. Planes bombed in the square made by the four hulks and there was a railway to take targets out. Lighters have been sunk along the coast to try and stop coastal erosion by wave action.

2. In 1949 marshes were filled in for the building of the Bradwell Nuclear Power Station. The baffle was built in the area where the sea bream and bass breed.

3. Bradwell Waterside. From 1850-1932 the Parkers, a Bradwell farming family owned forty barges which included the ones they had bought up from their rivals Goymer of Bradwell and Mizzen of Foulness. In the Edwardian period Clem Parker had twenty-six sailing barges in the stackie trade to London from the Blackwater and Colne creeks and the Outfalls along the Dengie coast. Local legend is that Parker's barges left Bradwell Quay loaded and went around the south end of Pewit Island. Parker died in 1932 and his barges were sold off. The creek here is much deeper than it was before the 'Great Flood' of 1953. Peter's Creek, named after a boy who was drowned here, at the south end of Pewit Island has also become deeper. About a dozen moorings here in 1960 rose to 150 in 1993.

4. In order to try and safeguard the Blackwater oyster fishery which was the largest of the Essex native oyster grounds, the river between West Mersea and Bradwell was leased to the Fish and Oyster Breeding Co in 1867. After this company collapsed the Tollesbury and Mersea (Blackwater) Oyster Fishery Co (known as T & M Co) took over and in 1878 employed about 260 men and up to 70 smacks. In the 1930s numbers of oysters, probably due to increasing pollution, declined rapidly but the company kept going by leasing out moorings to large merchant ships. Serious oyster production stopped after 1962-63 hard winter killed most of the oysters. The T & M Co has been doggedly kept going by families with long associations with oyster cultivation.

5. The Orplands Marshes were flooded with salt water in 1995 by the National Rivers Authority. It was hoped this would encourage wildfowl.

6. Ramsey Island is also known as Ramsey Wick and Stone Point. About 1870 the Wade was walled of so the Ramsey became part of the mainland. During World War II a landing hard built on the point. This was used by Stone Sailing Club which by the early 1960s was one of the leading dignhy racing clubs on the east coast.

7. Maldon Several Fishery. Maldon District Council owns the River Blackwater above a line between Wade Creek, which once divided Ramsey island from Stansgate Point, and the Rebank on the Gore saltings. In 1995 most of the Several Fishery were leased to the Essex Oyster & Seafood Co.

8. Stangate Abbey. Cluniac priory founded in 1176.

9. Mayland Creek. In 1868 the Mayland miller George Cardnell was operating six sailing barges from Mayland Creek, mostly from Pigeon Dock at the head of the creek. James Cardnell took on this fleet and had Howard build him the barge *Mayland* in 1888.

10. Lawling Creek. In the 1920s property developers began dividing the fields and orchards into a new resort called Maylandsea Bay. Yacht building yard of Cardnell Bros established here in the 1930s. During World War II the Admiralty put in the concrete apron to enable Cardnells to build 122ft B Class Fairmile motor launches. In 1994 the yacht yard was extended and pontoons added to create the Blackwater Marina.

11. In 1832 J.Marriage of Mundon had a mile and quarter canal dug from the mouth of Limbourne Creek up to White House Farm. Lighters brought 15 tons coal which was intended to be cheaper than shipping it through Maldon.

12. In 1991 Ron Hall won an award for research that lead to the recognition that the stakes on the mud near Cooper's Creek were the remains of late Anglo-Saxon fish traps. His first finds were the extensive ebb tide traps on The Collins which were the largest fish traps in Britain. These traps, including those at St Lawrence Bay, The Nass, Mersea, St Peter's Point and Foulness appear to date from about 940–990.

13. Hilly Pool Point. In 1772 234 acres of saltings were enclosed to create grazing marshes on Northey Island. The walls were breached in 1887 and returned to saltings. The farm house and barn were destroyed by bombing in World War II and the present house was built by the Nobel Prize winner Sir Norman Angell who owned the island from 1923-47. Angell gave the island to his nephew E.A.Lane who gave the 286 acre island to the National Trust in 1978.

14. Because the increasing number of brent geese were causing serious damage to winter wheat on the Blackwater marshes a 'goose field' was started on Northey in 1982. This encouraged some two thousand geese to feed here. In 1994 a small piece of river wall beside Southey Creek was removed to reflood grazing marsh to attract more geese.

15.The Stakes. Causeway over to Northey Island, possible site of the Battle of Maldon in 991 when the Anglo Saxons tried unsuccessfully to beat back the raiding Vikings.

16. Inlet where smacks used to lie until about 1895 when the Bath Wall was built to create a swimming area. About 1928 the Promenade was built along the wall. There was a rope walk for making cordage and rope at the end of Hythe Quay. The present Hythe Quay was built up in the Victorian period and a flat chalk berth laid for the barges to lie alongside.

17. Town Hard.Just down stream was The Shipways which was probably where the 50 gun 556 ton frigate *Jersey* was built in 1654. Early nineteenth century collier brigs and schooners built here. Between 1879-1912 John Howard built sailing barges, smacks and yachts here. Howard lived in the house at the bottom of North Street with the design office next door. About 1901 Barr, Payne and Hocking had the yard and built the barge *Columbia* and the smack *Joseph T* . In 1921 Dan Webb reopened the old Howard yard for building the 18-20ft Blackwater sloops. Later became Dan Webb and (Jack) Feesey.

18. Up steam of the free Town Hard was Tom Hedgecock's yard. He ran pleasure boats from the beach below Maldon Promenade. In the early 1990s 'Noddy' Cardy revitalised the yard by digging yacht berths and building jetties.

19. The Sadds gave the Downes to the town so that the children of Maldon would have somewhere to play. Rest of the Downes was divided into building plots, but Charles Barker moved from The Shipways to turn three plots near the river into the Downes Road boatyard. Charles Barker built the 44ft smack yacht *Betsan* in 1931 and remained at the yard until he died in 1951. Dixon Kerley next operated the yard. In 1979 a group of Blackwater sailing people bought the yard to prevent it being turned into houses. Brian Kennell and Arthur Keeble were rebuilding and building wooden boats here in 1995.

20. In 1812 the course of the river was straightened to wash the silt away from the Maldon wharves. 1865 Maldon Harbour Act allowed the river to be dredged deeper and straightened from Fullbridge to Heybridge Basin allowing Maldon to develop as a port. Many warehouses at Fullbridge. Shrimp Brand Beers were delivered by sailing barges to a warehouse which still has their motif. In the 1960-70s Brush ballast barges loaded at the wharf below the bridge.

21. The Causeway originally crossed the open marshes between Maldon and Heybridge. In 1994 a 40 acre site north of the Causeway was excavated and found to have been an Iron Age settlement, then a Roman town followed by Anglo-Saxon occupation. Heybridge was the important medieval Blackwater port, but by the sixteenth century Maldon, due to the changes in the channel, became more important. After the Blackwater was straighten and the Chelmer Navigation built, Heybridge was cut off from the tidal water. The shallow Heybridge Creek is all that remains of the old channel.

22. Heybridge Basin constructed in 1793 for ships to discharge coal, corn and timber for the Chelmer and Blackwater Navigation. In 1928 Hans Kuijten started a business importing Danish and Dutch eels here because the water was cleaner than the Thames where eels had been imported for centuries. The eels were discharged into lighters off Osea until the trade died out about 1968. Herring's Point was Metes Point and renamed after farmer Herring. In 1960 Brush built a ballast loading berth so that craft did not have to wait for the tide to get up to their Truman's Wharf, Fullbridge. Barge *Lancashire* was sunk to become a jetty for a three legged crane.

23. In 1974 Arthur Holt and James MacMillan started building wooden boats here. This is on the site of Mucker's Island named after 'Mucker' Clark who around 1900 lived on the island in a house known as Rat Hall.

24. Around 1900 Joseph Going ran a shipyard here complete with slipway, blacksmith's shop and sail making loft. Taken over by May & Butcher who by the late 1940s were shipbreaking here.

25. Salcote Creek. There was a salt works here until 1825. Their warehouses were converted to a maltings. Ancient burial mounds, the Barrow Hills were levelled when the Salcote Maltings were built about 1880. Howard built the barge *Salcote Belle* in 1895 for the malster Fred May to replace the *Star*. The last freight from Salcote Mill was taken away by the barge *Centaur* in about 1952.

26. Mill Beach. Heybridge Tide Mill which lasted until about 1920 trapped its water in the pond behind the riverwall. Brigantine *Robert Adams* had ports cut in her side so that Baltic timber could be discharged on the beach here.

27. Causeway to Osea. David Cole bought the 333 acre Osea about 1965, sold it in 1972 and then bought it back six years later. The island's farm was laid down to grass for brent geese in 1989.

28. Bawley Creek. This was the farm wharf for Osea.

29. Charrington built the mansion house on Osea about 1910 and the pier. He also built the chapel and sanatorium (converted to flats as Charrington House in 1992.)

30. Goldhanger Creek. Stackie barges loaded here with hay and straw from as far away as Tiptree. Wreck is the stackie barge *Snowdrop* which was brought here when no longer used as a Heybridge timber lighter.

31. Site of one of the four duck decoys which once operated between Decoy Point (Fauley Point) and Mell Creek. In the ninetenth century wildfowl were trapped in winter to sell on the London markets. The river walls on this section of the Blackwater are lined with Essex blocks which do the very important work of holding back tidal water.

32. Button's Beach with a summer house.

33. Around 1900 the farmer Richard Seabrook had three stackie barges working to the Thames from his wharf at Skinner's Wick at the head of Thirslet Creek. Also an area known as The Lost Field which was being farmed until it was flooded in the 1920s.

34. The Pacific oysters fattened off Gore Saltings from about 1991.In the winter about 2000 brent geese feed on the mud flats here at low tide. In the late winter when their food has been exhausted they move to the farmland.

35. Site of Tollesbury Pier. In 1907 the Kelvedon & Tollesbury Light Railway Company opened this pier and station which was intended to attract yachts from Brightlingsea to have moorings here. Not successful and remains of the pier pulled down in 1951.

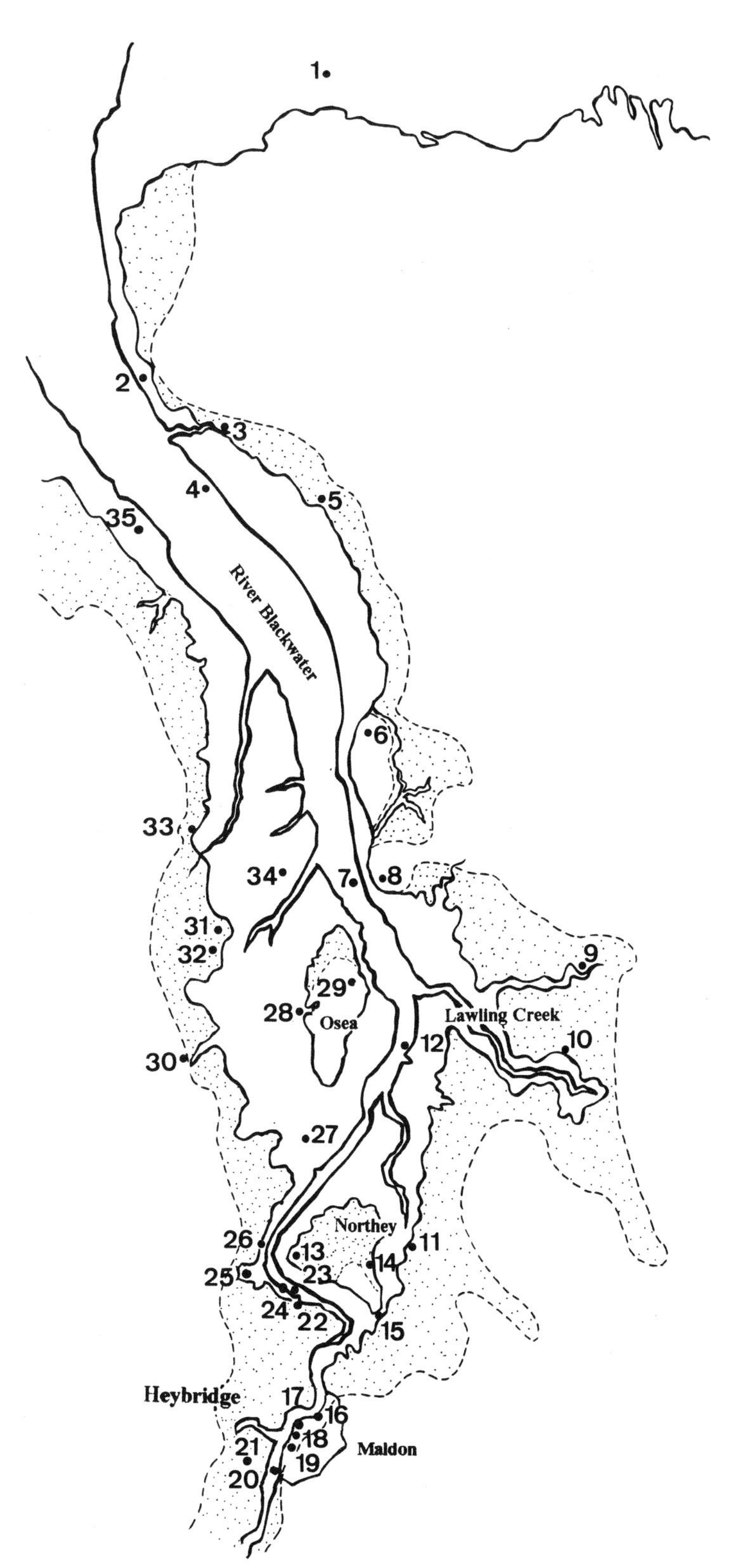

Chapter Five

THE CROUCH, ROACH AND THEIR ISLANDS

Above. 111. A smack racing at Burnham in about 1913. From medieval times until the coming of yachting oysters were the main industry on the Crouch. The oyster cultivation ended abruptly after the hard winter of 1962-63 when the stock of native oysters were killed. Since then there have been only a few wild oysters in the Crouch and some fattening of Pacific oysters.

Below. 112. Irene Booth, wife of the Bosun, on the Burnham schooner *Cateran* in 1911. Although the river below the Roach was mined during World War I this clipper bowed schooner remained in commisson taking out servicemen from hospitals. She became a houseboat at Burnham in 1918.

113. J.W.Patterson and Fred Pitcher on the starting balcony of the Royal Burnham Yacht Club in 1921. The Burnham Yacht Club was founded in 1895 and held its first race two days after.

114. Launching of the *Firechest* at R.J.Prior and Son, 1959. On the left is Reg Prior and on the right the yacht owner Lennie Danual and Murray Prior.

In 1892 John Prior started the business on Burnham waterfront as a coal and oyster merchant. The coal came in from the north of England by sailing barges and the oysters were cultivated in the river in front of the coal wharf. John Prior also built a three storey yacht repair workshop at Buckingham Square. In 1933 John died and his son Reg took over running the business and started yacht building. Before World War II Priors were building about one yacht a year but after this they became one of the leading yacht builders in England and produced many well known wooden ocean racers and cruising yachts.

The last wooden hulled yacht built by Priors was the cold moulded West epoxy half tonner *Harmony* in 1980. After this the yard produced glass fibre hulled yachts and provided storage and did repairs. Reg's son Murray took over and in 1982 his son Robin joined the firm. In the 1980s property boom the Priors resisted selling their site in the middle of Burnham water front. They believed that in the long term yacht building was better for them and their employees than a quick buyout offer.

115. Lowering the engine into the 45ft oyster smack *Vanguard* after she was built by Priors at Burnham in 1936. By this time the Prior's coal business had finished but their yacht moorings were still removed every autumn for the winter oyster dredging.

116. The largest vessel launched by Priors at Burnham was the 72ft research vessel *Lalla Rookh II* in 1957.

117. The work force of R.J.Prior at Burnham after the launch of *Lalla Rookh II* . The Prior family are on the right.

118. The 41ft Holman-designed *Cervantes II* just before her launch from R.J.Prior & Son (Burnham) Ltd in 1965. She was typical of the superb one off wooden yachts produced at this yard. The yard often had six yachts under construction at the same time from drawing boards of the leading designers of the day such as Kim Holman, Robert Clark, Olin Stephens and Jack Giles. However Alan Buchanan moved into Priors houses on the water front just after World War II and designed the majority of the yachts built here.

119. Launching of a 48ft ferro-cement ketch by Ferro Cement Marine at Burnham in about 1972. Mike Harris, John Hobson and Colin Baker rowing. At the time the great yachting boom had just taken off on the east coast and there was a tremendous demand for new yachts. As wood had become far to expensive there was a major movement on the Crouch to use ferro cement as a cheaper replacement.

120. The ferro gaff cutter *Skua* at the Colne Race in 1978. She had been built by Mick Wilkinson at North Fambridge and launched the previous year. This was one of a series of ferro cement hulls built in the meadow between the 'Ferry Boat Inn' and the river wall. 'Mick the Brick' Wilkinson went on to build more ferro cement boats on traditional lines on the Crouch, in Cornwall, Ireland and returned in 1991 to Tollesbury to build a 28ft lugger .

121. In 1987 the Old Gaffers Association challenged the Royal Cornishthian Yacht Club to a race to see whether the gaff or bermudian rigged East Coast One Design was the fastest. Here Arthur Keeble in his gaff *Chittabob IV* is finishing just ahead of the bermudian *Joyce*. The 30ft *Chittabob IV* was built to G.U.Laws design in 1913.

Left. 122. Aboard the motor barge *Ethel May* bound up to Battlebridge in 1960. On the left is the huffler Cresswell and on the right skipper Barry Peace. The river pilot, Mr Cresswell did not have his own boat and had to be picked up at Burnham.

Below. 123. Jack Coote sailing his pride and joy, the Dragon *Cluaran* , which was the last boat this well known yachtsman owned. From 1956 until his death in 1993 he wrote the editions of *East Coast Rivers* , the cruising guide to the east coast estuaries. His daughters Janet Harber and Judy Jones are continuing on with the series.

124. Inside Havengore Creek about 1965, a photograph by Jack Coote. The working smack on the right has a basket aloft which is normally only hoisted when a vessel is trawling.

125. View about 1970 from Jack Coote's *Blue Shoal* in Little Wakering Creek at high water. On the left is Little Wakering Church. After Jack Coote moved to Rochford about 1960 he based the double ended centreboarder *Blue Shoal* and other yachts at Paglesham.

126. A hard winter at Paglesham about 1959. This view of the saltings by Janet Harber is in the Essex coast tradition of atmospheric photographs in black and white.

127. The River Roach in the summer, about 1959. This photograph sums up the atmosphere of Essex rivers. The river wall against the skyline, saltings, and the ooze with a gaff yacht peacefully at anchor.

128. Stambridge Mill at the head of the River Roach in about 1958 with their barge *Lord Roberts*. The original timber building on the left has since been burnt down. The mill was owned by the Rankin family from 1838 until 1962. In the first half of this century A.M.Rankin Ltd owned two sailing barges, *Joy* and *Lord Roberts*, which brought imported wheat from the Royal Docks, London. Each barge loaded about 120 tons and took about a week on a round trip. The *Joy* was sold to become a yacht in 1952 and the *Lord Roberts* was then fitted with an engine and went on trading as a motor barge until about 1963.

129. A sailing barge at Stambridge Mill with the thatched Broomhill barns in the background.

130. Mo Deal towing the *Cambria* up to Stambridge Mill. During the 1960-70s most coasters were bringing in wheat from Rotterdam, but in 1968 there was a poor harvest in Britain which lead to the mill having to import wheat from the Baltic. This wheat came to the Baltic Wharf in the Crouch and smaller barges brought it round to Stambridge. The *Cambria*, then the last barge trading under sail, was amongst the barges on charter for this lightering.

Mo Deal took over from Snappy Noakes as the Leigh pilot in 1962 and became the Roach pilot between 1966-89. When taking a loaded coaster up the twisting channel the coasters often touched the edge of the mud, but their weight carried them forward and they often went over at an alarming angle until they slipped back into the channel. The greatest difficulty was with ships being moved light in strong winds because being high out of the water they were often blown ashore in the twisting channel. It often took several days to get down to Paglesham. Mo Deal used to have a tug which pulled the vessels head to keep her in the channel.

131. Captain Alan Pratt's *Locator* at Stambridge Mill. The early 1980s was a very active time for shipping at Stamford Mill because Canadian and USA wheat was being brought in, and animal 'Wheatfood' was being exported to northern Europe. In 1984 the mill switched to using English wheat for flour making but only one freight came up in the *Severnside* in the first six months. However that summer there was a poor harvest in England and after this three coasters were busy bringing imported wheat. The largest ship up here was the *Wilks* drawing 10ft 6 ins with 750 tons.

132. The Danish coaster *Joel* on the inside berth was a regular trader to Stambridge Mill until 1986. The *Subro Viking* was loading 'Wheatfeed' for Amsterdam. Ships can only be swung round at Stambridge Mill after they have been discharged.The strikes by the London dockers forced trade out from the Thames into the small Essex ports. Once during a dock strike in 1968 there were fourteen loaded ships laying at anchor at Paglesham. At Stambridge Mill four ships were being discharged every twenty four hours and the wheat taken by road to Tilbury

133. A view from Stamford Mill shows how the coasters coming up scoured the cant edge and kept the channel open. The crane on the right was for lifting timber out on Sutton Wharf. After 1988 the upper Roach was buoyed and Alan Pratt brought his own ships up.

134. White weeder in Barlinghall Creek, 1993. White weed is a type of coral which grows in sheltered parts of the sea bed and is dredged up, dried and sold for decoration. This trade started on the Dutch coast in the Friesland Islands in about 1930. There was also one man working a skiff white weeding from Leigh in the 1930s. About 1948 fishermen working hand hauled rakes started harvesting white weed in the Thames Estuary and by the early 1950s this had developed into a local gold rush. This was mainly centred on Leigh, but boats from Mersea to Canvey Island joined in the white weeding boom and it was so lucrative that some men sold their houses to buy boats.

The practice of dragging two huge rakes on wheels along the sea bed evolved and these were hauled on deck by power winches. In 1994 twenty four boats were white weeding in the winter from Essex ports. Most of these were based at Leigh and Southend, but six worked from the Crouch and Roach. The Mersea men only joined in if the fishing was bad.

135. Tony Judd on his Leigh cockler *Alice* & *Florrie* after passing through the Havengore Bridge in 1993. The creeks between the island near the bridge almost dry out at low water, but the shallowest part of the Havengore passage is crossing the Maplin Sands to join the Thames Estuary.

135A. The two sailing barges at Battlesbridge must be waiting to load a 'stack' because they have their small stackie foresails bent on. Behind the barges bows two lime kilns can be seen. There was a small creek running behind the quay up towards the 'Barge' pub but this was dammed off from tidal water.

135B. Stambridge Mill, Rochford in about 1908. The barge on the left is in the 'brick berth'. The head of the river has slowly silted up here.

THE RIVERS CROUCH, ROACH AND THEIR ISLANDS

1. Foulness. The largest of the five Roach marsh islands. There were Romano-British settlements on Foulness and the name means 'Headland of the birds'. Most of the island was reclaimed in the seventeenth century by the Dutch. Some of these men stayed as tenant farmers and introduced arable farming as it was good land. In the early nineteenth century this remote island attracted criminals on the run. The farmers did not live on the marsh islands, but employed foremen and brought in gangs of Irish labourers at harvest time. In 1805 and again in 1833 river walls were built to extend Foulness Point. The sinking of wells, fourteen by 1889, led to a more stable population of around 750 people. In 1855 the War Office started a firing range at Shoeburyness and as guns improved the Army wanted a longer range. In 1914 Alan Finch, Lord of the Manor, died and after this Foulness and the Maplins were purchased so that the Army had a 12 mile range from Shoeburyness. At first Foulness remained open to the public, but when a firing range was established here it was closed. Foulness had about 150 residents in 1975 and compared to the rapid urbanization of the rest of south east Essex is quiet and remote.

2. The Broomway. A five mile road between Wakering Stairs and Fisherman's Head, on the Maplin Sands. This was the link for Foulness and Havengore before the road bridge was built, but it could only be used at low water.

3. Old oyster storage pits on Potton Island beside Middleway. New England Creek was dammed up about 1922 to join up New England and Havengore islands.

4. Potton Island. In the 1880s wheat grown here was shipped away in sailing barges. Only one tree on the island and all fresh water brought in barrels. In the late Victorian agricultural depression the island was put down to grass for cattle and sheep and in the early 1940s ploughed up again for wheat. Private ferry to Potton until the road bridge was built about 1965.

5. Havengore Bridge. First lifting bridge and concrete road was built in 1922. Present bridge 1988.

6. Rushley Island. All drinking water had to be taken across in barrels until the first 500ft well was bored in 1829. Rushley, Potton and Foulness are controlled by the Ministry of Defence and closed to the public.

7. Millhead. Rutter's sailing barges loaded at their brickyard here. As many as twenty barges remembered lying 'wind bound' in the Parlour, a small mud harbour. Last barges sold about 1942.

8. Barlinghall Creek. Sailing barges used to load at wharves above the present landing. The World War I concrete lighter is said to have been brought here by the oyster men in the 1930s. After World War II Gilsons of Southend tried to revive the oyster fishery by fattening imported oysters. In 1972 a cleaning plant was installed, but mainly used for cockles. Until about 1960 a landing craft used to bring cockle shells from Foulness to Barling Hall. In 1993 six boats were white weeding from Barlinghall Creek.

9. The Violet. The old oyster ground at the mouth of Potton Creek.

10. Oyster grounds from Barling Ness to Barton Hall were used in the early 1980s for fattening imported oysters.

11. Roper's Wharf. Old farm wharf once used by sailing barges.

12. Barling Wharf. Meeson's schooner *Glencoe*, before she was lost in 1882, used to deliver coal from Sunderland and Newcastle to Barling quay on neap tides and to Stambridge on spring tides.

13. Sutton Wharf. In 1964 this wharf was built to bring in Baltic timber because the dockers strikes were paralysing the Port of London. Later builder Roy Carter extended the wharf by sinking World War II concrete lighters and filling over them. Ballast was shipped in from Southwold in the early 1970s. Because the coaster needed a high tide at each end it was too slow and uneconomic. Carters built the slip for their own yachts. Very shallow off here, some coasters take three tides to reach the mill.

14. Hunter Yachts started in 1970 and in early 1990s turned out about hundred grp hulls a year.

15. Hard bottomed dock built during World War I for building concrete ships. Reputed to have been used to repair submarines in World War II.

16. Brick Berth. Until about 1914 sailing barges loaded bricks at a wharf opposite the old mill which were brought down by a narrow gauge railway. Local boatmen say the head of the Broomhill River is silting up.

17. Stambridge Mill. In the mid Victorian period 100 ton barges took flour to the Thames wharves for the London bakehouses. Until about 1980 Hubert and Alf Keeble used to go out in a launch from Paglesham and pilot ships up to Rochford. Coasters of 200-300 tons came up every fortnight on the big tides.

18. Black Shed was once the only land mark on the landscape of river walls at Eastend, Paglesham. Between 1855-75 Kemp built sailing barges and oyster smacks in the Black Shed. The first shed blown down in 1881 gale. James Shuttlewood, who was an apprentice here in 1877 when the barge *Paglesham* was built, took over from Hall in 1896. Shuttlewood built the barge *Ethel Ada* here in 1903. His son Frank Shuttlewood continued building with craft such as the Leigh cockler *Unity* in 1948 and the barge yacht *Tiny Mite* in 1956. Frank died in 1965 and the yard was bought by the Norris' who sold it in 1989.

19. Oyster storage pits all along the Eastend shore and up into Paglesham Pool. Because the tide into the Broomhill river, above Paglesham, has two entrances from the Roach and Havengore there is little movement in the water so that the young oyster spat is not washed away. This made the Paglesham area a successful oyster fishery.

20. At Paglesham, locally 'Peglesham', the oyster grounds were along the mainland shore. In the Victorian period great fortunes were made culivating oysters in the Roach and its creeks. In 1900 twenty eight smacks and 140 men worked for the Roach Oyster company, but this started to decline in 1914. In 1977 Norman Childs restarted the Paglesham Oyster company on the grounds above Paglesham Pool. About 80 tons of oysters were sold each winter and the Paglesham Oyster Festival was very popular. Fishery closed and the smack *My Alice* sold about 1987 after the disease Bonamia hit the fishery.

21. Paglesham Pool. Old oyster storage pits on the creek and behind Wallasea Island. In 1995 there were Pacific oysters being fattened here in crates.

22. King's slipway and sheds were put up to build the 90ft yacht *Moonbeam*. Workmen came across the river from Burnham on a ferry. Several large yachts built here and sheds were used for storage. Last of the sheds blown down in 1981.

23. In the 1920s Wallasea Bay Yacht Station was started. Yachtsmen came by rail to Burnham and crossed on the Creeksea Ferry. From 1945-78 a ferry brought workmen across from Burnham. A regular ferry service from the Town Steps restarted in 1993. In the 1987 Hurrican most of the yachts and pontoons in Essex Marina were blown across the river. After this the pontoons were secured by posts.

24. Wallasea seems to have taken its name from Wall Fleet the old name for the Crouch. Good farmland. The drinking water was brought over from Burnham until artesian wells were sunk on Wallasea in the 1920s. In 1930 Davey & Armitage were operating the Baltic Wharf to import timber. In the 1953 Floods all the Crouch and Roach islands were submerged, two people drowned on Wallasea and three on Foulness.

25. Creeksea Ferry Inn. A rowing ferry over to Creekside operated by Albert Cottis until about 1935. There was a bell on the Creeksea hard and this area is still called The Bell.

26. Old oyster storage pits with shed. Upper Lion Creek was dammed up about 1955. This cut off Lion Wharf and left the Ramsgate smack *Problem* trapped inside. The Old Fleet continued on from Lion Creek and nodoubt used to join up with the Crouch near Upper Raypits barns in the Easter Reach. Until about 1954 the barge *Persevere* was running cockle shells, loaded by wheelbarrow at Fishermen's Head, Foulness, up to the oyster shed.

27. In 1016 the Danish King Canute defeated the English King Edmund Ironside at the Battle of Assandun, presumed to be Ashingdon, placing England under Viking domination. According to legend the Danes won because they took the position at the top of Beacon Hill. Legend says that the famous incident of King Canute ordering the tide not to come in, took place at Creeksea.

28. South Fambridge had an RAF seaplane repair base in World War II.

29. Brandy Hole. In the eighteenth century smugglers who were being chased by the Revenue cutter sank brandy here attached to blocks of salt. Later when the salt dissolved the packages of brandy surfaced.

30. Meeson's Steam Mill at Battlebridge on the north quay built in 1897. In 1916 another mill was built on the south quay. These mills were sold to J. & G. Matthews in 1926. The mill on the south quay was burnt down and replaced by a new mill in 1933. Because the tide was out when a old mill burnt, a hole was dug in the channel to retain water. Probably the last vessel up with grain was the motor vessel *Peter Robin* in 1969. By this time the mill on the north side had become a granary, but the south mill was producing 8000 tons of animal feed a year. The mill closed in the 1980s and was pulled down while north mill became a antique centre.

31. Hull Bridge fell down in 1769 and was replaced by Battle Bridge at the head of the tidal water. This bridge collapsed when Sadd's steam traction engine went over it in 1871. The next bridge lasted until 1995 when it was rebuilt.

32. Tide Mill above Battlebridge road bridge was built in 1772 on the site of an earlier mill. In 1897 W.T.Meeson closed the tide mill and opened the new mill by the bridge. Tide mill pulled down in 1902, but the kiln and granary survived. Granary extended in 1977.

33. In sailing barge days two hufflers (river pilots) guided barges up and down to Battlebridge and controlled drifting on the tide by ropes temporarily made fast to posts and anchors.

34. Remains of a medieval bridge were still at Hullbridge in 1930 as well as barges wharves on both banks. Dick Hymans operated a rowing ferry between Hullbridge and South Woodham Ferries until 1948.

35. In the 1920s a wooden bridge across Fenn Creek to Eyotts Farm. It was local tradition that this had been built by French prisoners of war during the Napoleonic Wars. In 1889 the Eyotts Estate sold Fenn Meadow as a single plot and it was developed with hut sites. In the 1920s Country Homes Ltd, the 'Asbestos Kings', started building small wooden bungalows beside Fenn Creek.

36. 1898-1908 Woodham Ferris Brick Co had a jetty on the Champion Estate, Clementsgreen Creek to load bricks

37. Stow Creek. About 1974 work started on digging out the West Wick Marina. Expanded in 1994.

38. Longpole Reach. Marshes above North Fambridge were abandoned after the 1897 floods because there was an agricultural recession then. Bungalow out on the old wall used for isolation unit.

39. Fambridge Ferry. When the yachting writer Francis B. Cooke started coming here by railway from London about 1897 there were only two oyster smacks and a steam yacht based at North Fambridge. First club house was a tin shed which had been the store for the steam yacht's gear. Last ferryman Reg Watson finished in 1972 just as North Fambridge started to expand as a yachting centre.

40. Shortpole Reach. Oyster laying at Fambridge in 1790. Died out in 1950s and restarted in 1993.

41. The Smugglers. In Althorne Creek oyster grounds near the chalets of the Smugglers Club.

42. Bridgemarsh Island. There was a cottage and brick kiln on the island. About 1921 the river wall broke and flooded Bridgemarsh. 600 sheep were drowned and two hay stacks floated about the river until the engineers blew them up. The river didn't come over the wall, but it burst because of rabbit holes and poor maintenance. Abandoned after 1933 flood. Became wildfowlers reserve.

43. Hulk behind Bridgemarsh was the steam drifter *Girl Nancy* which was brought to Burnham in 1922 for conversion to a yacht.

44. No yachts between Bridgemarsh in 1960, but demand for yacht moorings led to floating pontoons being layed to create Bridgemarsh Marine.

45. Creekside Farm. In 1944 1500 soldiers and marines were billeted here in a massive camp as they prepared for the D-Day Invasion of Normandy.

46. Burnham Yacht Harbour for 350 yachts built in 1988.

47. In the nineteenth century the Burnham Oyster Co rented the river bed from the Mildmays, Lords of the Manor. The oyster merchants controlling this company built many of the big Burnham houses. Laban Sweeting built the clock tower in 1877, Augers built Warners Hall and The Lawn (demolished to make way for Belvedere) while the Hawkins built Cupola House (now Memorial House). The Smiths and Richmonds were also oyster merchants and owned barges which brought coal from the north of England.

48. After the railway reached Burnham, two London yacht clubs, the London Sailing Club and the Royal Corinthian Yacht Club moved here. In 1893 the two clubs held informal races and this progressed on so that Burnham became the premier yacht racing centre on the east coast. The Crouch is within easy travelling distance of Greater London and the wide open marshland allows a good sailing breeze.

49. Crouch Harbour Authority. In 1272 the whole River Crouch from the Ray Sands up to Clay Clodd (entrance to Clementsgreen Creek) was granted to the Manor of Burnham. The whole river remained in private ownership until the Crouch Harbour Authority was started in 1974.

50. Royal Corinthian Yacht Club house with its flat roof was built in 1931 on 38 concrete piles driven in the river bed.

51. On the old shoreline of the Dengie Marshes there are Red Hills which were created by Iron Age salt production. There were about 200 Red Hills in Essex, many now destroyed. They were dotted all over the Essex marshland, but were the most numerous along the Dengie marshes and the north shore of the Blackwater.

52. In the Elizabethan period the entrance to the Crouch ran north close along the shore in what is now the Ray Sand Channel. The Crouch's old name Wallfleet seems to have meant 'shallow river near the wall'.

53.In 1987 there was dredging near the Sunken Buxey Buoy to allow larger ships in, but the wharf needed for 450ft 10000 tonners was not built. In 1995 the average ship coming into the Baltic Wharf was 350ft long and drawing 16ft (5m).

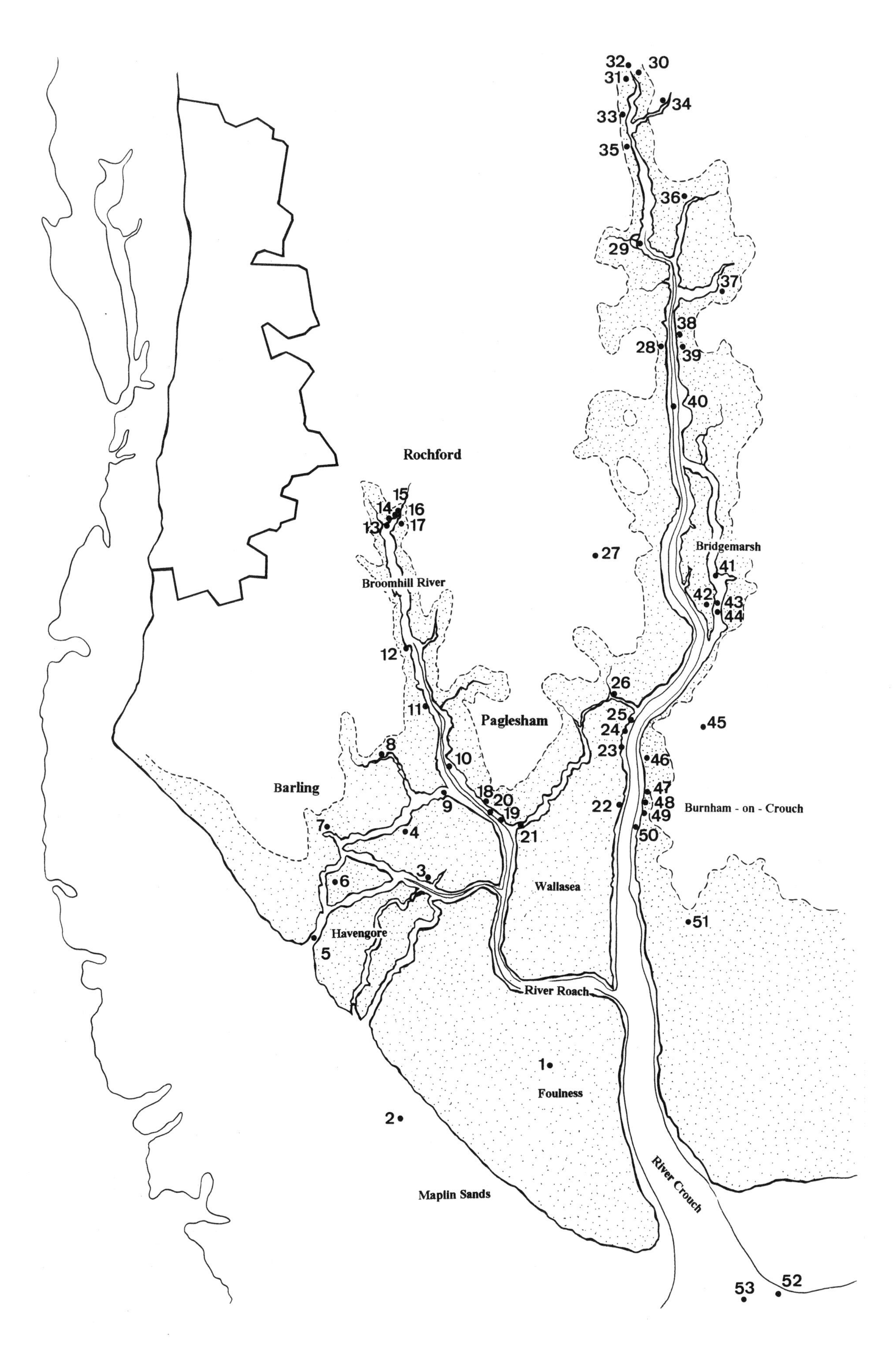
Rochford
Broomhill River
Paglesham
Barling
Havengore
Wallasea
River Roach
Foulness
Maplin Sands
Bridgemarsh
Burnham - on - Crouch
River Crouch

Chapter Six

THE THAMES MOUTH

136. Shoeburyness about 1913 with sailing barges in the background waiting to load bricks. About 1860 Josiah Jackson started brick making at Shoebury at the Shore Brick Field. Later another Model Brick Field was started further inland and then both fields were bought by Eastwoods. Most of the Shoebury bricks went away by railway. Sailing barges brought in coal and sand and took out corn and some bricks, brought down on a horse drawn railway. There was enough trade to this open beach for Shoebury to have its own barge building yard near Rampart Street. Here the *Shoebury* (1879) and *Scud*(1898) were built. Barges stopped coming on to the jetties in 1939 and brick fields lasted about another ten years.

137. Tripper boats landing on the Marine Parade beach at Southend-on-Sea about 1925. The larger pleasure boats ran trips round the Nore light vessel or over to Sheerness for a shilling(5p) a head.

138. Southend beach about 1910 with sailing pleasure boats. There was bitter rivalry between the men operating pleasure boats from the East and West beaches on either side of Southend pier. While the fishermen from Leigh were treated as hostile foreigners.

139. The centreboard Leigh cockle boat *Mary Amelia* ashore on the Maplin Sands about 1919. The cocklers ran on to the sands at high tide and when the tide went down the fishermen hand raked the cockles out of the sands and loaded up the boats.

140. Landing the cockles at Leigh about 1905. So many cockles were landed here that the old shells were taken away by sailing barges to be layed on the river bed for the Colne oyster fishery to make culch for the oyster spat to cling to.

141. The Leigh bawley *Bona* racing in 1904. After ending her fishing career converted to motor craft, the *Bona* was well restored back to her original sail plan. The bawley was the sailing fishing boat of the Thames mouth. They had a wide beam to give them stability so that when they returned home with the shrimps cooking, the hot water was not spilt from the copper. The bawleys went shrimping in the summer and after sprat in the winter. They carried a great cloud of sail because they normally sailed in sheltered waters and their beamy hulls needed extra power to push them through the water.

142. Cocklers in Leigh in 1935. Hand raking on the sands stopped after the Meddles fitted their *Ranger II* with a suction cockle dredger in 1967. The practice of men carrying the cockles ashore in baskets with shoulder yokes ended in about 1990.

143. The *Ceresta* at Old Leigh in 1980. The fleets of boats in Essex fishing centres declined after World War I but the Leigh fleet appears to have held its own. In 1890 there were 86 bawleys and 32 open cockle boats at Leigh, but the fleet reached a peak in the white weed boom in 1951 when there were 52 boats and 100 men after the weed and 44 boats and 118 men fishing. The original fishing village only became Old Leigh after a development company bought the farmland on the hill above it in 1893 and developed the new Leigh-on-Sea. After World War II the well meaning council thought that Old Leigh with its single street of old houses and warehouse had no place in a modern welfare state. They had already pulled down part of Old Leigh when in 1972 they decided to implement the post war plan of pulling down all Old Leigh and putting a new coast road to the proposed Maplin airport. James Wentworth Day, the great champion of traditional Essex, spoke out loudly and said that this 'wonderful jumble, part of the soul of England' had to be saved and after much local protest it was. However this corner of Essex remains in serious danger of loosing its local identity. People need houses but Spanish style villas look totally out of place in the green fields of Essex.

144. Mo Deal's tug towing the motor vessel *Contict* up to Theobald's Wharf, Leigh with beech bales from Le Treport in 1986. After the barge trade petered out in the 1960s the larger motor vessels continued using some of the smaller ports such as Leigh and Southend. The largest vessel to get up to Leigh was the 450 ton Danish *Procyon* in 1965, while the largest up to Southend in 1974 was a 600 tonner drawing 11ft 4ins.

Trade to the Gas Jetty at Southend stopped about 1963 and the last ship with general cargo up to Southend Loading Pier was about twenty years later. The last ship to Theobald's Wharf at Leigh was the *Doreen B* with beech bales in 1986. Ships outgrew these smaller ports.

144A. Pleasure boats leaving Southend with trippers about 1904. Most of these pleasure boats were built by Heywood at Southchurch beach. He launched the *Skylark* in 1886 for the Lilly brothers and the following year *Jubilee* for George and Alfred Myall. Then in 1888 Heywood launched the *May Queen* and *Four Brothers* and the largest of the sailing pleasure boats, the *Victoria* and the *Prince of Wales*.